Life Into Art

LIFE INTO ART

Isadora Duncan and Her World

Edited by Dorée Duncan, Carol Pratl, and Cynthia Splatt

Foreword by Agnes de Mille

Text by Cynthia Splatt

W.W. NORTON & COMPANY   NEW YORK   LONDON

Printed in Hong Kong

First Edition

The text of this book is composed in Cochin
with the captions set in Copperplate 31b
Manufacturing by South China Printing Co.,Ltd., Hong Kong
Book design and typesetting by Katy Homans and Sayre Coombs

Library of Congress Cataloging-in-Publication Data

Life into art : Isadora Duncan and her world / edited by Dorée Duncan, Carol Pratl,
and Cynthia Splatt ; foreword by Agnes de Mille ; text by Cynthia Splatt.
    p.   cm.
Includes index.
1. Duncan, Isadora, 1877–1927—Pictorial works. 2. Dancers—United States—
Biography. I. Duncan, Dorée. II. Pratl, Carol. III. Splatt, Cynthia.
GV1785.D8L54   1993
792.8'028'092—dc20
[B]   93-1737

ISBN 0-393-03507-7

W. W. Norton & Company, Inc., 500 Fifth Avenue, New York, N.Y. 10110
W. W. Norton & Company, Ltd., 10 Coptic Street, London WC1A 1PU

1 2 3 4 5 6 7 8 9 0

Frontispiece and small drawings in the margins throughout:
Pencil studies of Isadora dancing by Valentine Lecomte, Duncan Collection

Contents

AGNES DE MILLE

Foreword

Isadora Duncan died in 1927. By that time sound film had been developed, but not one foot of film exists of this great dancing, of our greatest original, and the pictures in this book—many never before made public—are therefore important.

Isadora started her career at the time of the held camera pose; there were then no instantaneous flashes, no twirls, no jumps, no falls, no quick expressions. She stands, she gazes, she yearns, but she does not balance, or hover, or take to the air in any way, and any fleeting or passing expression is lost. This tends to make her look a touch ponderous, which she may have not been at all.

There exist pictures of Ruth St. Denis in 1906 dancing a nautch, her extravagant skirt fluted out from her in swirls by centrifugal force. These appear to be instantaneous pictures. They were not. The points of the skirt were stretched and held out with threads while Ruth bent backward in the center and held miraculously still for the required long seconds of exposure. Similarly, the posed flight of Anna Pavlova was sustained by a strong and steadying male arm, and subsequently all evidence of the support was removed. Isadora made use of no such dodges. But Isadora never appeared to fly except in one double exposure.

From infancy, Isadora knew she was destined to be special. The youngest of four children, she was the leader, the instigator of all plans, and the most outspoken. She dominated the other three, kidnapped them, devoured them. They were brought up by their mother alone (the father had decamped) in a free-thinking, free-experimenting, wholly non-orthodox manner.

The Duncans thought of themselves as revolutionaries. America has always fostered cults. The nineteenth century saw many and many had to do with dress. Susan B. Anthony and the people who wished to obtain the franchise for women were considered a "cult." Dolly Bloomer and women's dress reformers were considered cultists. Sixty years later, Irene Castle got women out of corsets; Marlene Dietrich got them into pants.

They were each helped by a war and work opportunities subsequently opened to a new generation of women. Were these trivial reformers? No, they were basic. Isadora had wanted to get women into sandals and Greek robes. She did not succeed. She had seemed too odd, too special to copy, and women went down another path. They were now working in trades, in offices, attempting heavy physical labor in rough environs. Marlene simply showed them how to be pretty while following the new patterns set by necessity. Isadora did not and could not change the modes and manners of her time, but in her short life she modified its entire theatric aesthetic. Afterward we could never again revert to the patterns we had followed before her tearing and stripping away of non-essentials.

Isadora, like that particularly American phenomenon, Evangelical preachers, expressed herself best at the apex of exalted emotions. She prepared carefully, but at a moment of heightened stress she was by her own admission known to abandon all plans and deliver herself to the emotion of the crisis. And she admits (even perhaps boasts) of having danced long improvisations which became famous, on the spur of the event; the spontaneous first performance of *The Blue Danube* is a famous example of this exuberance. Everything she did or said was seemingly by impulse. And this explains her extravagances and her occasional outrageous claims. She did not think; she felt. She was certainly not always sensible and she was often irresponsible. She frequently borrowed money from her hard-working brother, Augustin Duncan, which he could scarcely afford to spare, and squandered the sums on expensive hotels, champagne, caviar. She obtained money from a friend because she was hungry and spent the lot on flowers. Which was daft. Her admirers thought it divine. Once in Nice a woman injured in a street accident was carried into her house. The bed happened to be covered with costly garments.

"Lay her here," she ordered instantly.

"Mind the clothes!" said the careful Frenchmen. "Move the clothes."

"No, put her down. Never mind the clothes."

The bloody, mangled body was dumped on the silks.

Isadora went to the heart of any situation, discarding all pretension, and it is on such heroic directness that her reputation stands. In her speech she was brave, outright, forceful, challenging, but seldom if ever humorous. Was she invariably either heroic or passionate? It does not seem likely or even desirable. But Isadora intimate or non-heroic escapes us. What a loss!

There is a photograph of Isadora standing in a long tunic before the Erectheum. Her stance is tranquil and enduring, and she waits, at one with her environment. Not so the stone figures above her, also standing, but not at peace, not waiting. They march. Their dynamism seems to shout. They pierce the centuries. The living woman fades back into the earth and sky and rocks. Isadora was a shattering iconoclast, but Isadora's face is never aggressive. It is a waiting face. Simply it is. She has the self-sufficiency of genius. She knows. She does not have to do anything. Fate will come to her.

In this stillness she differs from other dancers and all actors. The actor's face is mobile, a web of instinctive changes, reflecting back life in its entirety. It is seldom still; is various. Who is this individual, this personality? That depends. Does this mask reveal the inner dynamic being that instigates all the personality images? Can one know?

The face of the dancer, on the other hand, is still but it is not passive. All expression here is held in abeyance against the moment of total bodily release, when strength, dynamics, and energy will transform into action. Then the face may also move, but only to a minimal degree, and the force that would have expressed itself in an ordinary human by shouting or screaming manifests itself in the case of a dancer by extreme movement—for instance, great leaps, without, however, any distortion of the lips or eyes. All this is promised behind the dancer's waiting. Study the liveliness, the bewitchment, behind the masks of Anna Pavlova, Vaslav Nijinsky, Tamara Karsavina, Alicia Alonzo, Ruth St. Denis, Martha Graham, Mary Wigman. These are noble visages, still and beautiful, but shielding enough force to move a continent.

Not so with Isadora Duncan. In this instance a very great artist, an overpowering personality, photographs like a normal woman, a woman fulfilled and at peace with the world. The broad, placid forehead, the mild eyes, the chin drawn in without aggression, drawn in in modest-self possession, the meek, even shy chin, the sweet yielding mouth, bespeak patience, understanding, and, yes, conformity. The slightly tilted head, the diffident gaze reinforce the impression of vulnerability, even girlishness, and always susceptibility. Isadora looks like any female relative—perhaps a wife or mother, the successful head of a household or a beloved daughter.

But Isadora, we know, was none of these. She was a wild voluptuary, a true revolutionary. She flouted every tradition. She was the law-giver, Mosaic in her endeavor. She tried to enforce a new code of human behavior and was outspoken as few people have ever been. She alone and unhelped changed the direction of her entire art. She tried to change humanity; that she could not do, certainly, but she changed the viewpoint of a good part of humanity. Yet as we look at her mild womanly face, with none of the tightened discipline of the other great professionals, we must wonder.

Isadora's quiet visage was reinforced by the fact that she used a minimum of make-up, none at all in private life. Her deportment was modest. But the moment she spoke, her clear American voice rang out and the message sounded like trumpets.

And this mild-faced woman could mirror all emotions, all circumstances, all events. When young, Isadora was capable of light playfulness and blossoming grace, when older such horror-filled grief that grown women wept uncontrollably to see her. "Why do you cry?" I asked my mother, I myself being totally unmoved by her posturing and her somber, staring eyes. "Her children were drowned, and she seems so sad," replied Mother, not understanding anything Duncan was doing but recognizing, as did everyone in the audience, bottomless grief.

One looks at the whole figure. Ah, here is Diana, long-limbed and fleet! She had a girl's torso. Unlike other dancers', it soon became a woman's. The lovely ripe arms were very long, the legs and ample thighs long, her feet long and classic, not highly developed with flexible insteps like those of a ballet dancer or of Ruth St. Denis, who possessed enormous arches without training. Duncan's were coolly classic and as she wished them to be, light as leaves, or massive, set in stone. From her early teens she had the body of a dancer, and every lift of the hand, every inclination of the hand or knee, was lovely and meaningful. Isadora did not have to learn how to dance. She danced from childhood. What she had to learn was to understand men's hearts and minds and life. But from the very beginning she could move beautifully. One sees this in the pictures. Alas, it is true she did little to discipline her God-given body. By the time she was thirty, she had heavy arms and legs. At forty, she shook with fat.

Nor did her costumes help her. The Greek sculptors knew very well what they were doing, and edited, eliminated, revealed. The real Greek robes probably were bulky and formless, and it was from a shapeless mass of yardage that Isadora's matchless arms and speaking hands stretched, that her long, beautiful legs flashed, that her feet, bare before the world and God, touched earth and left an immortal mark. Although no doubt historically correct in all details (Isadora was a meticulous scholar), Isadora's earlier robes did not mold to her form like the classic robes of Phydias. She used white cotton or linen, which totally muffled her, until in 1900 she discovered Liberty silks. (The Greeks did not have silk.) Later she began using gauze and chiffon. She and her pupils evolved tunics of fluttering softness that moved subtly with the body's

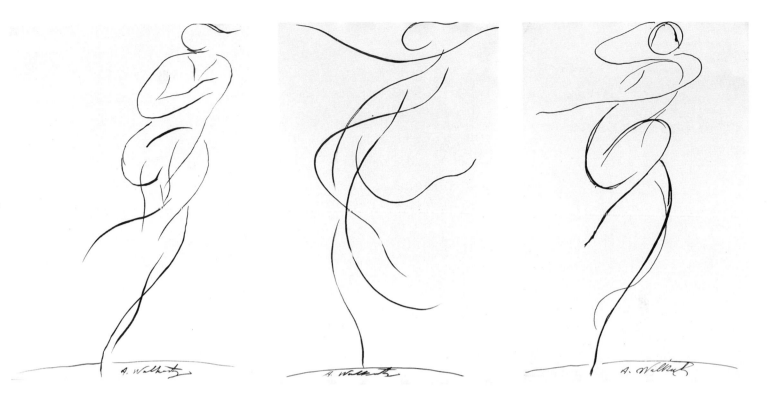

Line drawings of
Isadora dancing
drawn by Abraham
Walkowitz after her
death, 1932, Duncan
Collection

needs. It is in the later photographs that Isadora, the goddess woman, finally stands revealed.

But Isadora's costumes at the beginning were makeshift (in one instance consisting of a wrapped window curtain, and it is indeed bulky and ungainly). Isadora's body was ideal for dancing, permitting her to fall into classic attitudes, and she carried the stuffy garments nobly. But they were stuffy, and we have no pictures of the garments in motion; for any idea of how they looked in action, which is, after all, the way they were seen, we must go to the drawings, which are beautifully revealing. Here indeed Isadora dances—gossamer light, aerial, even playful, fairy feckless.

There are photographs of Isadora's children. Deirdre, the little daughter, Gordon Craig's child, has a soft and loving face. All of Isadora's womanliness has gone into her. She seems a touch stodgy, but that may just be baby fat.

Patrick, on the other hand, the son of Paris Singer, four years younger, although a baby, is well defined as a person. The very carriage of his head is determined—one wants to say, virile. For me, the most heartrending image in the book is the intent gaze of this son—golden, beautiful, unshadowed by any sadness or foreboding, so pathetically soon to be drowned in a hideous car accident. This face explains Isadora's bottom-

less, unending grief, her taking to drink. It also explains her exalted universal joy.

She took to drink in her late thirties. Her admirers excuse it by saying it was un-answerable grief at the loss of the children that caused this decline. At the end of her life Isadora tottered on the brink. When young and hopeful, the spirit turns on the fountain source; but when old, the springs fail and one is forced to rely on artificial help or banked energy.

The true quality of Isadora Duncan's dancing is shown in one double exposure which suggests her light and gracious turning, her infinite suggestion of faeriness. The Germans called her *die heilige Isadora* ("Holy Isadora"). Francis Biddle, our Attorney General, said to me once, "It's worth being old now just to have been young when she was and to have seen her."

No one forgot. She passed by and men knew greatness.

I did not see Isadora when she was young, but only in 1918 when she gave a solo concert in Los Angeles. I was a child and understood nothing of what I was watching, but whole phrases stick in my memory exactly, and although I did not at the time know the music, I later recognized it as Glück. For example, she lay on the stage and threw imaginary knucklebones, holding her fingers high to signify the tally. It was childlike and playful and memorably simple. She skipped in place in mounting crescendo. It was a real crescendo, trumpets sounded. She turned her back and summoned as she skipped in counter-direction, light, free, classically pure. There was something so childishly innocent, so essential about her gestures as to render them timeless, without history, the basic possession and hallmark of the human race. She summoned, we followed.

The concert I saw was during World War I. At the end of the performance, the entire audience rose and stood while the orchestra played the *Marseillaise*, the Allies' anthem, all six verses, and Isadora in long Greek robes and a blood red cloak danced. At the final call: "Aux armes, Citoyens, Formez vos bataillons," she threw her blood red robe over her shoulder, marched to the footlights, and confronting the audience raised her arms in heroic summons.

The whole house cried out, many people wept. She gave voice to immortal anguish, to mortal endeavor. Isadora could match any monument. She could match life. And yet at the time she was an overweight woman who at frolicsome moments seemed almost inept. Anyone else doing similar things would have been downright ridiculous. Isadora was never ridiculous. Isadora raised her arms and the stars rocked.

CYNTHIA SPLATT

Preface

Isadora Duncan: Her name evokes images of beauty and grace, passion and defiance, courage and tragedy. A legend in her lifetime and a myth since her death, for all her fame she is among the least known historical figures of our century. Countless people know her name, but most of them know little about her, beyond the fabrications of overly sentimental admirers or the slander of jealous detractors. Behind the mist of Liberty silk and Moët champagne stands an artist, a woman. Isadora Duncan was not a goddess, she was a human being, with weaknesses we might all see in the darkness of our inner mirror. What set her apart was the strength of her passion for art and the depth of her love for life, her imagination, her energy.

Isadora Duncan the artist belongs to the world. Her work is known and respected in France, Germany, and Russia to a degree that surpasses her fame in America. Although, like many artists of her generation, she lived much of her life as an expatriate, she was always profoundly American. Isadora wrote of her pioneer ancestors with pride and she exemplifies the traits that characterize Americans. Isadora was courageous, optimistic, hardworking, and generous. She had an almost childlike belief in the goodness of human nature and the rectitude of her own opinions. She had difficulty seeing the reason behind much social and political behavior. Isadora was an idealist who imagined a future where humanity would achieve its potential harmony.

This vision included beauty. She believed that humanity must have beauty—it was as necessary to life as air and water. For Isadora, "Art" was simply the label that language had affixed to the human expression of "Beauty." For her, Art sprang from the depths of the human soul, and though it might be an expression of joy or of sorrow, it was always noble and beautiful: *"Art which is not religious is not art, it is mere merchandise."* (*The Dance of the Future, 1903*).

Isadora Duncan's life work was to restore dance to its rightful place among the

15

arts. Dance was to be sacred—not an entertainment at best, a titillation at worst, as it had become in European and thence in American society. To accomplish this goal, she had to free the minds and bodies of women from the psychological and physical constraints placed on them by male-dominated societies. And she had to reeducate men regarding their perception of a woman's place in Art. She managed to do this gracefully, beautifully, without the anger of many of our contemporary female activists. While some might say that she was too gentle, no one can deny the lasting force of her work. Those who saw her dance—as a young lady with the face of an angel wearing only a wisp of silk, and as a tired, heartbroken woman, a mother with empty arms, dressed in wrinkled muslin—found her art utterly human and noble. She touched the most diverse souls and changed the way they regarded the female, body and soul.

The mother of Modern Dance and a pioneering feminist, Isadora Duncan discarded corsets and slippers and the theatrical conventions that cast women as victim or seductress. Seeking the source of true dance, she went back to the origins of the theatre, in early Greek religious ritual, where the dancer expressed human sentiment through movement. She developed a dance technique based on natural movement motivated by emotion, and she believed that the spiritual and physical center of the body is the solar plexus. It is this central placement that gives Duncan Dance its depth and force.

Isadora Duncan was the first artist to dance great classical music—Chopin, Beethoven, Brahams. She integrated instrumental and vocal music, spoken text and visual elements, with dance. She always maintained that the art of the dance was a part of the art of the theatre. Coupled with her revolutionary ideas, this widened the scope of her influence. Few artists of our century have influenced so many spheres of creativity. The world recognizes Modern Dance as an American art form, and Isadora Duncan as the artist who sowed the seeds.

Isadora is often seen standing alone in history. It is forgotten that she came from an extraordinary family, who lived and worked surrounded by a circle of friends comprising some of the great artists of our century. They inspired and influenced her, and she them—musicians, writers, poets, painters, sculptors, photographers, directors, actors, and technicians. Most of the pictures in this book come from the Duncan family collection. Many of them have never been seen; many more were published in the years following her death and have been largely unavailable or poorly reproduced over the years. It is a joy to share them and to show Isadora as her loved ones and her fellow artists saw her.

DORÉE DUNCAN

Acknowledgments

This book really began in 1978 when we all met at the Akademia Raymond Duncan. I had moved to Paris the day after my graduation from Harvard University to direct the Akademia, since my grandmother, Aia Bertrand, had died the previous year. The Akademia was composed of three sixteenth-century buildings in the heart of the art district in Paris. It had a publishing house, theatre, art galleries, lecture hall, weaving school, and much more. The second floor housed a museum dedicated to the Duncan family, first set up by my grandfather, Raymond, in the 1930s and then reformed to be the museum of the Four Duncans by my parents, William B. Seligmann and Ligoa Duncan.

I was in Paris to begin my life. I had been raised with immodest expectations: to forge new paths, to be independent and free-thinking, to never believe anything anyone said, to never care what anyone thought, and, most importantly, to be creative and ingenious. But nothing in my upbringing had prepared me to maintain a legacy and preserve the history of the works and lives of my ancestors. Rather lost with all these responsibilities, I concentrated on starting an English language theatre, which took up most of my time.

It was then that I met Cynthia Splatt and Carol Pratl. We became friends, our common passion being the theatre. Cynthia Splatt was writing a dissertation for the University of Paris on Isadora Duncan and Gordon Craig. She was also becoming the first woman and the first American to become a Provost of the French Academy of Arms. At this time I was hoping to enter the Paris-Dakar in my 1977 Mini Cooper. Cynthia and I exchanged lessons in standard foil and standard transmission in the Forêt de Fontainbleau. Carol Pratl had come to Paris right after finishing high school in Chicago. Incredibly independent and energetic, she taught herself French and studied Russian and Chinese at the University of Paris. She came to the Akademia and studied Duncan dance. We immediately became friends, both loving vodka and champagne and the spirited conversations they fueled. Her Russian studies took her to the Moscow theatre scene where she researched Isadora's stay and influence in Russia. She hunted for and found former pupils of Isadora's and the schools derived from Isadora's philosophy; never idle, she founded *Sphinx* magazine and organized the first International Women Writers Conferences in France and Russia.

By 1983, we all separated. Cynthia was home in San Franciso; Carol was in Paris and Moscow; and I was on another planet, in graduate school at Columbia University in New York. But we stayed in touch, full of ideas for future productions and plans. We convened in my apartment and spent long days and nights together: Carol meticulously classifying each artifact with equal attention, from theatre program to unpaid electric bill, Cynthia separating scores of Abraham Walkowitz drawings by the watermark on the paper, while I insisted it was time for us to stop and have a drink. That is how this book came into being, the three of us, knee deep in photographs, letters, and programs, during a particularly hot New York City summer. Friends would stop by to visit, just to be handed something to sort or read out loud, some excusing themselves from time to time to take a cold bath.

It was my dearest and oldest friend, Karen Auerbach, probably very tired of these tedious "parties," who suggested that we make a book. She was all too familiar with life at the Duncan's, having known me since 1969, and having spent many years at the Akademia. Karen, associate director of publicity at Norton, put us in touch with Mary Cunnane who mentioned that Duncan, Pratl & Splatt sounded more like a law firm in a Dickens novel than the authors of a book on Isadora. Nonetheless, the project was approved. Eve Picower, our editor, has yet been unable to get all three of us on the phone together. That is probably to her benefit. It was certainly difficult for her and we thank her for her kind disposition when she must have been totally exasperated. We thank Katy Homans, the designer, for such a splendid-looking book.

This book contains many photographs, none of which would be seen were it not for the generosity and help of many dear and close friends. Roberta Fineberg was photographing women writers in Russia and graciously agreed to do the copy work in Moscow and New York. Catherine de Maria, a New York photographer, printed all of Raymond's original negatives and everything else I could hand her, but when it was time to create the photographs to be used in the actual book she was working on a project "somewhere in South America." Karen Rusch, photographer extraordinaire, directed me to Kathy Kennedy whose studio, Kennedy Photo Works, was consequently flooded with cartons containing anything from large-format glass negatives to torn programs, all of

⩔

THE EDITOR WITH
HER PARENTS AND
GRANDPARENTS ABOARD
THE S. S. *LIBERTÉ*
(L. TO R.): LIGOA
DUNCAN, WILLIAM
SELIGMANN, DORÉE
DUNCAN-SELIGMANN,
AIA BERTRAND,
RAYMOND DUNCAN
PHOTO: 1960, DUNCAN
COLLECTION

COMPAGNIE SAN
FRANCISCO'S
PRODUCTION OF *VICTOR/
MARCEL DUCHAMP,*
CYNTHIA SPLATT'S
STAGE ADAPTATION OF
HENRI-PIERRE ROCHÉ'S
NOVEL, PLAYED AT THE
THÉÂTRE LE RANELAGH
IN DECEMBER, 1982.
CURTAIN CALL, *(L. TO
R.):* FÉLIX SCHÜTZ,
WILLIAM DOHERTY,
DORÉE DUNCAN,
CYNTHIA SPLATT,
FRANÇOIS LEVESQUE,
LIGOA DUNCAN, PETER
VIZARD, OLIVIER
HERMEL, BARBARA
CURTIN, CAROL PRATL.

which had to be printed immediately. Richard Hobbs invited me to one of his big dinner parties and later photographed the color artwork in the arrangements Cynthia and I devised on my mattress (which has the same aspect ratio as the pages in this book).

Uncovering valuable and new materials cannot be accomplished without the help and knowledge of those who are closest to the collections. We are indebted to the individuals at the Bibliothèque Nationale de Paris: Sabine Coron, Cécile Giteaux, and Nicole Laillet; Valery Gubin and Nelly Onchurova of the Bakhrushin State Theatre Museum in Moscow; Mme. Rhodia Duffet-Bourdelle of the Musée Bourdelle in Paris; Christian Larrieu of the Louvre Museum; my friends Elizabeth Orr of the Bettman Archive and Peter Dervis, another former Akademia inmate, of DHR. We extend our thanks to the International Dance Council of UNESCO, Judy Mings of the Woman's Heritage Museum, Leonid Belozorovich, Theodora Varvarigou, Natalya Dukhovny, Stuart Johnson, Olga Seminova, and to the late Irinia Lunacharsky.

Many people helped the Duncans without seeking recognition for themselves. This is a rare opportunity to thank them: Pierre and Bernadette Merle, Lucia Artopoulos Knowles, Ysé Richard Knowles, Pamina and Marc Missonier, Mildah Polia Pathé, Yvonne Hoenig, and, more sadly, to the memory of Jeanne and Jules Jailleu, Mitchell Salem Fisher, Edith Madwig, Fanny Robianne, Marc de la Roche, Docteur and Mme. S. Lebovici, M. and Mme. Kim Gaul Kwan, Mr. and Mrs. William Bradley, Mario Rosy, René Fauchois, Marie-Mathilde de la Roche Aymon, Julia McIver, Guillot de Saix, Fernand Divoire, Henri Heraut, Mrs. Sloan, Yvette Gilbert, and the lovely Chi-Chi.

These dancers have, each in their own way, endeavored to revitalize the memory of Isadora Duncan, and took the time to help us with this book: Lyle Almond, Vera

Belozorovich, Lucie Burkiczak, Janaea Rose Lyn Butler, Lois Flood, Mignon Garland, Barbara Kane, Madeleine Lytton, Odile Pyros, Kathleen Quinlan-Kritchels, Hannelore Schick, Shain Shödt, Madelyn Szepesi, Elena Terentieva, Quelita Trahan, Deborah Varnes, and Maria Villazana-Ruiz. Isadora's dances belong to the world, they are free for all to dance, let no one tell you differently.

Akademia life, first in Paris and then at the New York annex, has always been an extraordinary experience because of the people. I thank them all, but in particular Jerry and Irene Auerbach, who, whether or not they wish to admit it, have Duncan blood coursing in their veins; Elizabeth Chase Hecht and Bob Hecht for all the adventures; and Richard Meade, for protecting us from the evils of wicked governments. My dearest friends have been (and will always be) called upon to do one thing or another, ranging from running errands to enduring the transformation of casual dinner party conversation to long discussions about the preservation of the Duncan archives. I hope the memories are as dear to them as they are to me: Andrée Pagès, Linda Roux, Nicholas Heller, Amy Eller, Lee Comegys, George Foy, Alex Buchet, Charles Jay, Andrea Hecht, Alexandra Donici, Nancy Swartz, Elizabeth Mamatis, Judith Burnett, Christian Erikson, Donatella Hecht, Lynn Hoffman, John Edmark, May Pack, Sharon Fogarty, Tom Ellman, Josie Conte, Elizabeth Chapman, Jaques Robin, Frank Smadja, Yoelle Maarek, David Kurlander, Michael Elhadad, Axelle Said, and so many more. I must also thank my new visionary friends Sid Ahuja and Bob Ensor and colleagues Murali Aravamudan and Babu Ramakrishnan for their patience with my fractured focus on our new work. And finally, I must thank my dear brother, Michel Duncan Merle, who introduced me to the avant-garde.

But it is my parents who have demonstrated the greatest patience as they were continuously subjected to a steady bombardment of demands to identify people, find addresses, date events, and finally intersperse Duncan research and interviews with their international travel plans. Ligoa and Bill raised me as a citizen of New-Paris-York and always encouraged me on any path I might take. I have often found myself on more than one. That is a freedom for which I am eternally grateful.

This book is not intended to be a definitive text on Isadora Duncan. Her essence eludes definition; no one text could ever capture the totality of such a being. This book is written for those who can accept that, yes, a woman, independent, mother, artist, and thinker, did change the course of society, theatre, and dance simply through her own life. Isadora left her footsteps in the sand; they shift with time to fit the "youngest and the poorest," all those who would listen to the music of their own being.

Life Into Art

PART I

Lyrical: 1877–1903

Life is the root, Art is the flower.

— ISADORA DUNCAN, THE ART OF THE DANCE

In April 1906, the firestorm that followed in the wake of the great San Francisco earthquake incinerated all public records and swept away whole chapters of the city's history. Isadora Duncan and her family, living in Europe, happy and successful, might have breathed a private sigh of relief, thinking that some of their sadder memories had been purified by flame. The Duncans were San Franciscans and could have been one of the city's first families, but for some injudicious investing in a savings and loan venture.

Joseph Charles Duncan was the grandson of General William Duncan of Philadelphia, a veteran of the War of 1812, a successful merchant and a respected politician. Born in 1819 in Philadelphia to Harriett Bioren and Joseph Moulder Duncan, for a time his father was a professor of *belles lettres* at Washington & Lee University in Lexington, Virginia. The family later moved to Illinois, where Joseph Charles Duncan married Eleanor Hill. In 1842, he published a small literary magazine, *The Prairie Flower*. He was also involved in the meat-packing business and printed paper money, negotiable in his own establishment (ironically foreshadowing his later business adventures). In 1848 he moved to New Orleans, where he served as editor of the *New Orleans Crescent* (Walt Whitman worked as a printer for this paper). The Duncans traveled west in 1850 to San Francisco, where their fourth child was born. Later, Joseph divorced Eleanor.

Publishing seems to have been Joseph's great passion. He was the proprietor and editor of the *Globe* (in its various permutations: *Daily, Morning, Evening*), the *California Home Journal,* and the *Mirror.* His interest in the arts influenced his choice of secondary business ventures, and in 1854 he opened an auction gallery—the Chinese Salesrooms—and became a successful purveyor of oriental decorative arts. In 1871 he was a founding

member of the San Francisco Art Association with its free Art School. Unfortunately, Joseph also became involved in real estate and banking, two sectors of the economy that were, if possible, even more volatile a century ago than they are today.

Joseph Duncan married again. His second wife was Mary Isadora ("Dora") Gray, the daughter of Mary Gorman and Thomas Gray. A native of Ireland, Thomas Gray had fought in the Black Hawk War, with Abraham Lincoln, before crossing the county by covered wagon to settle in San Francisco, where he started the first ferry boat service across the Bay to Oakland. The Grays lost a son in the Civil War, but Colonel Gray returned home to serve in the California State legislature.

This prominent Catholic family must have been taken aback when their daughter Dora chose to marry a divorced Episcopalian thirty years her senior. However, they did not stand in her way. Indeed, the two families seem to have been friendly, for when Joseph organized the Pioneer Land & Loan Bank in 1869, Thomas Gray became its president.

Dora and Joseph had four children: Mary Elizabeth Bioren (always called Elizabeth), born in 1871; Augustin, born in 1873; Raymond, born in 1874; and Angela Isadora, born in 1877. Isadora was born on May 26, into what may already have been an unhappy home, for by October 8 that year her father's bank had collapsed. Five

days later on the 13th, Dora took her little daughter to Old St. Mary's Church, to be baptized. The parish register survived the fire in 1906 and there, in a brief Latin entry, we first meet Isadora.

The bank failure involved the entire family. Thomas Gray had been president in name only and, while in disgrace, faced no criminal charges. However, Joseph's partners in the Pioneer Bank and its affiliate, the Safe Deposit Company, were his son by his first wife, William T. Duncan, and his son-in-law, Benjamin F. Le Warne. Even as William Duncan stood beside Dora Duncan as Isadora's godfather, his father and brother-in-law were evading the police. They were successful until the following February.

Joseph Duncan was finally arrested in a rooming house in San Francisco, Benjamin Le Warne in Oakland. After four trials, Joseph was acquitted. Indeed, it seems possible that other prominent men, including the mayor and well-known industrialists, were involved in his schemes. Today Joseph Duncan would pay fines and begin a best-selling book, but in 1880 his reputation was ruined, at least for a time. Dora Duncan divorced him and he moved to Los Angeles, where he embarked on a third marriage and a new career in real estate.

About her father, Isadora wrote mostly of absence, perhaps because even so many years later the truth was painful. In fact he seems to have maintained contact with the family over the years. During a period of success he moved them into a large home—an arrangement that did not last long, on account of his ever-fluctuating fortunes. And there is correspondence with Raymond indicating that he hoped for his son's participation in his last venture, the representation of the California Gold Mines in London. It was on a trip to England in October 1898 that he perished, with his wife Mary Cuppola and their little daughter, in a shipwreck off Falmouth.

Bret Harte's *Outcroppings*, a book of California verse, included a poem by Joseph Duncan:

INTAGLIO

Lines on a Beautiful Greek Antique

On the temple-crowned summit
Breaks again the rising day,
Streaming with its dawning brightness
Down the waters of the bay!

See, the centuried mist is breaking!
Lo, the free Hellenic shore!
Marathon—Plataea tells us
Greece is living Greece once more

Joseph Duncan's children studied the art and literature of ancient Greece, which for Isadora and Raymond was truly living and became a part of their art. But for many years before they set foot in Greece they would study, with their mother, a wide range of music and literature. Living on the free Californian shore, they developed the basis of an American art form that would contribute to the transformation of the European theatre. Messengers from a young culture, they would carry their brightness back to the Old World.

Dora Duncan was a woman of remarkable courage. For a young lady to divorce her husband and raise her four small children was as unusual as it was difficult in 1880.

Soon after the bank failure, their large home on the northwest corner of Geary and Taylor streets in San Francisco was sold to pay creditors and the family moved to Oakland. Over the next few years they moved repeatedly, unable to pay the rent on one dreary lodging after another. It is easy to imagine Dora's pain, and Isadora remembered the shame of being the poorest child at school. Elizabeth was sent to live with her grandparents for a while, but Dora kept the younger children with her and earned their living by teaching piano and knitting baby clothes.

Yet in spite of their financial poverty the Duncan children had a rich home life, a wealth of love and beauty. Dora filled the house with music. Isadora remembered her grandmother dancing jigs and Augustin remembered her reciting Shakespeare. Their mother's sisters were interesting, too. Augusta—Aunt Gussie—danced and encouraged their "theatricals"; Elizabeth—Aunt Lizzie—had foreign exchange students as guests in her home in Santa Clara. The children learned that the world was much wider even than San Francisco, full of people with unusual ideas, people who didn't have time to point fingers at those whose lives were different. So the young Duncans grew into an independent clan, fiercely proud and loyal to each other.

In 1885 the Duncans were living in a small but pleasant house in Oakland. Dora organized a social dancing class for the children and their friends, and played the piano while Professor Massbaum taught them waltzes and polkas. The young Duncans soon found a practical application for their lessons; by 1889, Elizabeth had established herself as a teacher of social dancing, and Raymond and Isadora soon joined her in the venture.

At about this time Isadora, then eleven years old, decided that school was a needless encroachment on her time and, as she put it, "pinned up her hair." Isadora loved learning—she was a voracious reader, and she never ceased to inquire and study; but traditional education and rote learning belonged to a different sphere from the one in which she moved. Ina Coolbrith, the poet laureate who was a librarian in Oakland, became her accomplice, guiding and encouraging the young girl's reading. Isadora had studied French and German seriously enough to be able to communicate once she arrived in Europe, and her tastes in philosophy and literature were decidedly advanced.

In 1905, Isadora wrote a "SKETCH of CAREER of ISADORA DUNCAN, up to the year 1903." This document is written in the form of draft program notes. It reads, in part,

Danced first as a small child—Studied from age of four years—Began to teach "a new system of body culture and dancing" at age 11 years.

Taught from the age of 11 years to 16 years—classes always growing—gave performances appearing both alone and with pupils—dancing singly and in chorus—and also the pupils danced and mimed small scenes—of mimodramas accompanied by Poems. The dancing of these pupils was considered wholly remarkable and something as quite opposed to the dancing of the time—Press of that time wrote expressing admiration for this New Dance.

At age of 14 made a tour of Principal Theatres of California—immense enthusiasm all along the route—

Danced alone—& also appeared in Combined dances with two brothers and sister.

If Isadora learned nothing else, she had certainly learned how to write a rousing press release; but this was not a total fantasy. In addition to social dancing, the Duncans were teaching aesthetic or fancy dancing, and their pupils gave recitals. Augustin was the director of the theatrical troupe they formed. Isadora made her public debut in 1890 in a recital at Wendte Hall, at the First Unitarian Church, on 14th and Castro streets in Oakland. She was thirteen years old, and all five Duncans performed together.

In 1893 Joseph Duncan installed the family in a new home, the former Castle mansion in San Francisco. The house and grounds afforded the young teachers and performers the luxury of space, and they profited from it to expand their classes and produce a

program which they took on tour along the coast. In 1894, Isadora Duncan appeared for the first time in the San Francisco city directory as a Teacher of Dance.

What was she teaching? What was this "new system of body culture and dancing"? She had learned social dancing and had some ballet training. Isadora's own research was initially inspired by the work of François Delsarte (1811–1871), a teacher of singing and declamation in Paris whose students included the greatest lyric and dramatic artists of the day. Researching human expression, he studied physiology and psychology to find a correlation between emotional stimuli and movement and utterance, and began to teach a "science of applied aesthetics."

In 1869 a young American actor, Steele MacKaye, went to Paris and became first a disciple and then a collaborator of Delsarte. At the outbreak of the Franco-Prussian War in 1870, MacKaye returned to New York, where he established a "Conservatoire Aesthetic" and School of Expression, hoping that Delsarte would soon arrive; unfortunately the master died the following year. Delsarte was not only a conscientious scientist but a deeply religious man, and the mysticism and Christian humanism that underlay his theories appealed greatly to nineteenth-century Americans. His influence on the performing arts in America has been inestimable, and his work became the cornerstone of a new tradition as America developed its own art of dance.

In March 1898, *The Director* published an interview in which Isadora stated that Delsarte, "the master of all principles of flexibility, and lightness of body should receive universal thanks for the bonds he has removed from our constrained members. His teachings, faithfully given, combined with the usual instruction necessary to learning to dance, will give a result exceptionally graceful and charming."

Two points of Delsarte's theories probably guided Isadora toward her emphasis on the solar plexus in expressive movement: the performer, using gesture and movement, should be inspired by emotion; and the body should be divided into zones governed by intellect, emotions, and senses.

"The Delsarte system" influenced thousands of other young Americans. It was responsible for the trend toward teaching corporal expression in primary and secondary education. The Grecian dance and physical culture classes to which ladies and girls flocked at the turn of the century produced few artists but opened the eyes and minds of a generation. Isadora hoped that the general public would adopt beauty and freedom as guiding principles in everyday life: "Woman is to learn beauty of form and movement through the dance." Of the several hundred children whom she personally taught to dance, only a handful became professionals, but the rest were no less important to her. She taught children to dance as much for life as for art. In 1927, she wrote:

People have never understood my true aim. Far from wishing to develop theatre dancers, I had hoped to train in my school numbers of children who through dance, music, poetry and song would express the feelings of the people, with grace and beauty. — "REFLECTIONS, AFTER MOSCOW"

When Isadora began to perform and teach in 1890, she also began her search for true dance. At Ocean Beach in San Francisco, where the streetcar line still ends, walk a few feet and you are standing in Isadora's footsteps. As she said in *My Life* (1927), "My life and my art were born of the sea. My first idea of movement, of the dance, certainly came from the movement of the waves. . ."—And again in "The Dancer and Nature" (1905): "Of all movement which gives us delight and satisfies the soul's sense of movement, that of the waves of the sea seems to me the finest. . . ."

> *I opened the door to nature again, revealing a different kind of dance, some people explained it all by saying, "See, it is natural dancing." But with its freedom, its accordance with natural movement, there was also design. "Natural" dancing should mean only that the dance never goes against nature, not that anything is left to chance.* —"MOVEMENT IS LIFE" (1909)

There were many representations of Grecian poses and mixtures of spoken verse and pantomime set to music, such as Isadora describes in the early performances of the Duncans' pupils in California. What ultimately separated Isadora's work from the rest of this popular genre? She always maintained that if the positions seen in her dances seemed Greek, it was because the Greeks had danced naturally, as she did, and that she had found the same positions through contact with nature. Her movements did not

derive from copied poses, but from the movement of nature—the waves of the sea, the trees blowing in the wind. Walk on wet sand—it is firm and supple. Stand on the seashore and feel the force of the wind, and it is quite clear what she meant.

This then was the basis of the "new system of dance" which Isadora was developing when she and her mother left San Francisco in June 1895.

Dora Duncan and her eighteen-year-old daughter arrived in Chicago with twenty-five dollars and a little jewelry, so it was not surprising that Isadora soon accepted an engagement to dance in the vaudeville show on the Masonic Temple Roof Garden. She was grateful for her paycheck but declined an offer of a tour. Instead, she obtained an audition with the great producer Augustin Daly. Daly had a theatre in New York and another in London, and a company of actors for whom he adapted European plays and Shakespeare's comedies. Isadora felt that her concept of dance would interest him. Indeed, he was impressed by her talent and hired her immediately. For the next several years Isadora worked with some of the leading actors of the time, including Ada Rehan, in a varied repertory.

Her first role was in a pantomime, *Mme. Pygmalion*, starring Jane May. After touring with this production for two months, Isadora was cast as the First Faerie in *A Mid-*

Summer Night's Dream. She was vexed by having to wear gauze wings attached to her costume: she wanted to dance her wingedness. She danced in *Much Ado About Nothing* and played a spirit in *The Tempest*. In *Meg Merrilies*, adapted from Sir Walter Scott's *Guy Mannering*, she performed a Gypsy dance.

In 1897 she went on the company's English tour. While in London, Daly arranged for her to study with Katti Lanner, the principal dancer of the Empire Theatre. Isadora never spoke about this training, or about her lessons in New York with Marie Bonfanti, another great theatre ballerina. Her dance was already quite different from that of the theatre in which she was working. As always, Isadora took the best of the past and carried it forward into the future.

Isadora had given some private recitals successfully in London, and when she returned to New York the following year, she decided to leave the Daly Company and work independently so that she could put her own ideas on stage. She created a number of dances, many of them accompanied by poetry. Her musical tastes were eclectic: Strauss waltzes, Mendelssohn, Paderewski, Nevin. Ethelbert Nevin had a studio in Carnegie Hall, and so did the Duncans. When he saw Isadora dance to his *Ophelia* and *Narcissus*, he asked her to join him in his next recital. Later Isadora spoke with regret of

Nevin's early death in 1901 and the loss of an American composer whose music she could dance.

Isadora was becoming a fashionable salon performer. Her mother played the piano, Augustin and Elizabeth recited, and sometimes Raymond would lecture on the philosophy of the dance.

On March 24, 1898, at the Carnegie Lyceum, Isadora joined Nevin in three *Water Scenes*. The program included a soprano and an actress. The recital received scant but polite press coverage, a brief item in the society notes. This typified the reaction of even sophisticated New York to dance. Music was art, but dance was entertainment. Isadora was accused of being "absolutely and painfully refined." Yet a year later, when she gave a recital with the playwright Justin McCarthy reciting, her dances on the *Rubáiyát of Omar Khayyám* managed to shock some of the socialites in the audience.

What on earth was she doing? When Isadora danced her *Rubáiyát*, people were alarmed—to a turn-of-the-century audience, bare arms and a dress arranged from her mother's lace curtains were daring. Yet it was really the dance that was more daring than the dress. The movement was different from anything seen on the stage at that time. Still wearing tights and satin slippers, she danced on pointe and on the high half pointe, which she would continue to use and to teach. But her center of balance was

higher than the ballet's traditional top-of-the-pelvis placement. Her arms, legs, and shoulders were soft. Her head tipped back, on a gracefully curved neck—a position she had seen on Greek vases, not in a ballet class.

These movements were not meant to tease or excite the audience, but to illustrate a whole range of human emotion inspired by the poetry and the music. Isadora wrote that at this time she was studying the music of Glück (whose resurgence in France and America was due largely to Delsarte's influence), and gaining an understanding of the relation between the movement of the Chorus and the force of tragedy. The Dionysian ideal was already guiding her work, as is evident in a statement she had made in 1898:

This is what we are trying to accomplish, to blend together a poem, a melody and a dance, so that you will not listen to the music, see the dance or hear the poem, but will live in the scene and the thought that all are expressing.

Isadora's nice-but-naughty lace curtains were consumed in a blaze that changed the Duncans' lives. On St. Patrick's Day, March 17, 1899, the Windsor Hotel, where they lived and where Elizabeth and Isadora conducted social dancing classes, caught fire. The Duncans, who were giving a lesson at the time, managed to lead all of their young pupils safely out of the burning building, but their own possessions were lost.

Having nothing left in New York, they decided to move to London. Augustin had

❧

THE DUNCAN FAMILY'S
FAREWELL APPEARANCE
IN THE UNITED STATES
BEFORE LEAVING FOR
ENGLAND WAS THE LAST
TIME THEY ALL
PERFORMED TOGETHER
IN THEIR HOMELAND

been playing Romeo and had married his Juliet, but the rest of the family were determined to leave as soon as possible. They gave a farewell recital on April 18. *The Happier Age of Gold* elicited the usual uninformed comments from the critics, but these same dances would soon draw the interest of a different audience in London.

Unable to afford even steerage class, they traveled on a cattle boat. (The sufferings of the beasts in the hold inspired the Duncan family's vegetarianism.) As Isadora had already worked and studied in London, they were greeted upon arrival by friends Isadora had made during her previous tours with the Daly Company. These friends in turn introduced them to prominent members of the artistic community. Isadora and Raymond spent every spare moment in the British Museum, studying the Greek antiquities, and in the picture galleries before the paintings of the masters.

Mrs. Patrick Campbell, the great actress, introduced them to Mrs. George Wyndham, who invited Isadora to dance at her home. One of the guests was Charles Hallé, the painter, son of the German pianist and conductor Karl Hallé. Charles Hallé was the director of the New Gallery, and he arranged a series of recitals there in 1900.

At the first recital, in March, the classical scholar and poet Andrew Lang spoke on Dance in relation to Greek Myth. Texts read by another classical scholar, Jane Harrison, included the Homeric *Hymn to Demeter* and the *Idylls of Theocritus*. A small orchestra, conducted by Mr. J.E. Barkworth, played music that included Mendelssohn's *Spring Song* and Nevin's *Water Nymph*.

The second recital, on July 3, was introduced by the composer Sir Hubert Parry, speaking on the illustration of Music by the Dance. The Countess Valda Gleichen sang the aria "Piango il mio ben cosi" from Glück's *Orpheo* and Isadora danced the ensuing Minuet from the opera. She also danced a Chopin Prelude, Waltz, and Mazurka. This program is of special importance as it marks the formal debut of dances to the music of two composers who were to inspire an important part of Isadora's repertoire for years to come.

The third recital, on July 6, focused on fifteenth-century Renaissance paintings, and the artist Sir William Richmond spoke on Botticelli and the *Primavera*. Isadora's dances evoked *La Primavera*, and the *Angel with a Viol* by Ambrogio de Predis, to the *Nobilitata d'Amore* by Cesare Negri, and *Bacchus and Ariadne* by Titian to the music of Giovanni Picci. J. Fuller-Maitland, the musician and critic, accompanied her on the harpsichord.

Clearly, Isadora's own work matured greatly that year, and between research and

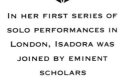

IN HER FIRST SERIES OF
SOLO PERFORMANCES IN
LONDON, ISADORA WAS
JOINED BY EMINENT
SCHOLARS

choreography she also found time to appear in R.F. Benson's Shakespeare season at the Royal Lyceum Theatre. She danced in the French camp scene in *Henry V,* in *The Tempest,* and once again in *A Midsummer Night's Dream.* The Lyceum was home to Henry Irving's company, and when she was not performing, Isadora would watch the work of this great Shakespearean actor and his leading lady, Ellen Terry. Another lifelong friendship began that year when Isadora met the young poet Douglas Ainslie.

Raymond had gone to Paris and was urging Isadora and his mother to join him, so later in the summer of 1900 they crossed the Channel. Charles Hallé accompanied them and together they visited the Universal Exposition. At the Exposition the Duncans saw the works of Auguste Rodin for the first time. A revelation of another sort was the work of the American dancer Loie Fuller and her guests at the theatre she had erected on the fairgrounds. Fuller produced spectacular effects, using colored lights shining through a transparent stage floor to illuminate her voluminous costumes of fine silk. She transformed herself into flames or flowers. Her movements were quite simple, but she was a master of scenic effect. She also had excellent taste and an appreciation of varied forms. She was sponsoring the great Japanese tragic dancer Sado Yacco and his company, and Isadora returned repeatedly to watch this dancing tragedian.

They went to see Mounet-Sully in the Comédie Française production of Sophocles' *Oedipus Rex.* They were thrilled by the great voice, but their moment of joy came at the end of the second act:

Mounet-Sully dances. Ah, here was what I had always envisaged—the great heroic figure dancing...How little did I ever dream that one day I would stand on that same stage with the Great Mounet-Sully.

For Raymond and Isadora, the Greek tragedy held endless fascination. They went to the Louvre and began an exhaustive study of the antiquities there, as they had done in London. The collection of tiny clay Tanagra figures of ordinary people performing ordinary motions particularly excited Isadora. Isolated, the act of fastening one's sandal strap or scarf had a special beauty.

The Duncans settled in a studio at 45, avenue de Villiers. Raymond draped the walls and painted Greek columns at intervals. Isadora wrote that it was here that she "discovered" her solar plexus. In London, she had moved from ballet slippers to sandals for dancing. Now she was barefoot. Her year in London had deepened her understanding of music. J. Fuller-Maitland had spoken to Isadora about the importance of the use of rubato in the music of Chopin. She was also working on more choreography to the

dances in Gluck's operas of the Greek tragedies. And there was the growing assurance of her technique.

Isadora's dance is often wrongly perceived as having no technique, as being simply the result of inspired improvisation. The fact is that Isadora had received traditional dance training, but she had questioned it. She retained much of the physical discipline of classical ballet, but she sought to use the resulting bodily strength to produce free, curvilinear movements emanating from the solar plexus:

> *I spent long days and nights in the studio seeking that dance which might be the divine expression of the human spirit through the medium of the body's movement. For hours I would stand quite still, my two hands folded between my breasts, covering the solar plexus. . . . I was seeking and finally discovered the central spring of all movement, the crater of motor power, the unity from which all diversions of movement are born, the mirror of vision for the creation of the dance.* — MY LIFE

Isadora also pondered the relation of dance to music. In the patterned choreogra-

ISADORA REHEARSING
IN THE DUNCANS'
STUDIO, 45, AVENUE DE
VILLIERS, PARIS
PHOTOS: RAYMOND
DUNCAN, PARIS, 1900

phy of ballet, the steps were set to music. In her own technique of dance composition, the movement grew out of emotions evoked by the music, or the movement evolved — beginning as emotions expressed by gestures in silence, for which she would then select music that illustrated those same emotions.

> *. . .I on the contrary sought the source of the spiritual expression to flow into the channels of the body filling it with vibrating light — the centrifugal force reflecting the spirit's vision. After many months, when I had learned to concentrate all my force to this one Center I found that thereafter, when I listened to music the rays and vibrations of the music streamed to this one fount of light within me — there they reflected themselves in Spiritual Vision, not the brain's mirror, but the soul's, and from this vision I could express them in dance.*
>
> *I also then dreamed of finding a first movement from which would be born a series of movements without my volition, but as the unconscious reaction of the primary movement. I had developed this movement in a series of variations on several themes — such as the first movement of fear, followed by the natural reactions born of the primary emotion or sorrow from which would flow a dance of lamentation or a love movement from the unfolding of which like the petals of a flower the dancer would stream as a perfume.*
>
> *These dances were without music, but seemed to create themselves from the rhythm of*

some invisible music. From these studies I first attempted to express the Preludes of Chopin. I was also initiated [in]to the music of Gluck. — MY LIFE

This was the principle of Delsarte reversed. Not to reproduce the movement that expressed an emotion, but to seek the emotion that would prompt that movement. But always, Isadora believed that the body must be ready to serve the soul, it must be supple and strong.

27 JUIN 1903

Before returning to London, Charles Hallé had introduced Isadora to his young nephew, Charles Noufflard. He and his two friends, Jacques Beaugnies and André Beaunier, the writer, adored Isadora and shared her company with no hint of jealousy. Beaunier's mother, Mme. St. Marceau, held a renowned salon on Friday evenings. She invited Isadora to dance there in January 1901. This led to a series of other invitations, including one from the Countess Greffuhle and one from the Prince and Princesse Edmond de Polignac. The Polignacs were patrons of the arts, the Prince himself a musician, the Princesse an American, and they opened their salon to the public, thus presenting Isadora to a larger audience.

One artist who saw Isadora dance at the Polignacs' was the painter Eugene Carriére (1849–1906). He spoke at one of her own studio recitals, saying, "The dance of

42

Miss Isadora Duncan is no longer an entertainment: it is a personal expression; as a work of art it is thus more living, and perhaps therefore more fertile in inspiring us to the work for which we are ourselves destined." Isadora often visited the painter at his home in Montmartre, appreciating his fatherly concern and the warmth of his loving family.

The works of Auguste Rodin had so impressed the Duncans that Isadora and Raymond also went to visit him.

In March 1901, Isadora gave a recital at the Palais des Beaux-Arts in Monte Carlo, and in July she returned to London to present another series of recitals at the New Gallery. *The Dance Idylls of Isadora Duncan* were presented on three separate evenings: "Dances inspired by Greek Art," "Dances inspired by Early Italian Art," and "Dances inspired by Modern Music." These performances were greatly appreciated by the artistic community. But Isadora was not receiving any commercial contracts in London, or Paris, and so when Loie Fuller invited her to join a tour of Eastern Europe, she accepted.

Fuller presented Isadora in Vienna and in Budapest. When the Hungarian impresario Alexander Grosz saw her, he had the good taste and the good sense to realize that

her dancing was more than entertainment, but also that it would appeal to a much larger public than just artists and intellectuals. He offered her a contract for a month at the Urania Theatre in Budapest.

On April 19, 1902, she opened to huge audiences and wonderful reviews. That spring was to bring a more personal triumph as well: her first love affair. Isadora met Oscar Beregi, an actor from the National Theatre, who played Romeo offstage as well as on. Their affair was passionate and tender, but it became rapidly apparent that Miss Duncan was not ready to abandon her career to become Mrs. Beregi. The romance ended, yet the love would endure; even after Isadora's death, Beregi corresponded with her brother Augustin.

Isadora went on to conquer Germany. In Munich, Grosz succeeded in booking her into the Künstler Haus and her success was enormous. The art students behaved like extras in an operetta: they unhitched the horses from her carriage and drew her home personally after each performance. Even those conservatives who objected to her dance recognized its merits. Berlin was next, and there she appeared at Kroll's Opera House. Again, opinion was divided, but no one who saw her was indifferent.

An editorial in the Berlin *Morgen Post* asking, "Can Miss Duncan Dance?" drew a

DORA DUNCAN, WALTER
SCHOTT, AND ISADORA
IN HIS STUDIO. HIS
SCULPTURE OF ISADORA
STANDS BEHIND THEM.
PHOTO: BERLIN, 1904,
DUNCAN COLLECTION

ISADORA'S MANIFESTO *THE DANCE OF THE FUTURE*, TRANSLATED AND INTRODUCED BY KARL FEDERN

ISADORA DUNCAN
DER TANZ DER ZUKUNFT
(THE DANCE OF THE FUTURE)
EINE VORLESUNG

ÜBERSETZT UND
EINGELEITET VON
KARL FEDERN

VERLEGT BEI EUGEN DIEDERICHS LEIPZIG 1903

witty reply from Isadora, "Can the Dancing Maenad Dance?" The maenad was, of course, the beautiful Greek statue in the Berlin Museum which, as she pointed out, had been "dancing in Berlin some years before Miss Duncan." Her letter gained her an invitation from the Berlin Presse Verlin to lecture. Her talk, *"The Dance of the Future,"* was published as a pamphlet; it became the manifesto of Modern Dance and a feminist classic:

> *The movement of the waves, of winds, of the earth is ever in the same lasting harmony. We do not stand on the beach and inquire of the ocean what was its movement of the past and what will be its movement of the future. We realize that the movement peculiar to its nature is eternal to its nature. . . .*

> *The primary or fundamental movements of the new school of the dance must have within them the seeds from which will evolve all other movements, each in turn to give birth to others in unending sequence of still higher and greater expression, thoughts and ideas. . . .*

> *My intention is, in due time, to found a school, to build a theatre where a hundred little girls shall be trained in my art, which they in their turn will better. In this school I shall not teach the children to imitate my movements, but to make their own, I shall not force them to study certain definite movements, I shall help them to develop those movements which are natural to them.*

There will always be movements which are the perfect expression of that individual body and that individual soul: so we must not force it to make movements which are not natural to it but which belong to a school.

The dancer of the future will be one whose body and soul have grown so harmoniously together that the natural language of that soul will have become the movement of the body. The dancer will not belong to a nation but to all humanity. She will dance not in the form of a nymph, nor fairy, nor coquette but in the form of woman in its greatest and purest expression. She will realize the mission of woman's body and the holiness of all its parts. She will dance the changing life of nature, showing how each part is transformed into the other. From all parts of

CELEBRATION IN HONOR
OF RODIN'S ELEVATION
TO THE RANK OF
COMMANDER OF THE
LEGION OF HONOR.
JUNE 30, 1903, VELIZY.
RODIN IS STANDING TO
THE LEFT OF THE
COLUMN SUPPORTING
THE WALKING MAN.
ISADORA IS SEATED ON
THE GRASS, AT LEFT.

ISADORA DANCING AT
RODIN'S PICNIC
PHOTOS: LIMET, PARIS,
1903, MUSÉE RODIN.
© MUSÉE RODIN

*her body shall shine radiant intelligence, bringing to the world the message of the thoughts and
aspirations of thousands of women. She shall dance the freedom of women. . . .*

*This is the mission of the dancer of the future . . . she is coming, the dancer of the future:
the free spirit, who will inhabit the body of new women; more glorious than any woman that
has yet been; more beautiful than . . . all women in past centuries: The highest intelligence in
the freest body!*

Isadora's speech received a great deal of publicity and there was an outpouring of
support for her ideas. She had established the art of Modern Dance.

In May 1903, Isadora returned to Paris to give a series of concerts at the Théâtre
Sarah Bernhardt. The public and press were less wildly enthusiastic than in Germany,
but the reaction of the art students was as warm. She gave complimentary tickets to the
students at the Ecole des Beaux-Arts, and among the young artists who saw her were
some who would chronicle her art in the years to come.

In June there was a picnic in the woods at Velizy near Meudon to celebrate
Rodin's elevation to the rank of commander of the Légion d'Honneur. Kathleen Bruce,
the sculptor (she would later marry Captain Scott) was one of the guests. She writes

ISADORA AT THE LIDO
IN VENICE, DANCING
ON THE WET SAND
PHOTO: RAYMOND
DUNCAN, ITALY, 1903

THE DUNCAN FAMILY
AND THEIR FRIENDS
LUNCHING AT THE LIDO
PHOTO: ITALY, 1903,
DUNCAN COLLECTION

ISADORA OUTSIDE THE
MUSEUM IN ATHENS

ISADORA AND KATHLEEN
BRUCE READING IN THE
MUSEUM, ATHENS

ISADORA INSIDE THE
MUSEUM, ATHENS
PHOTOS: RAYMOND
DUNCAN, GREECE, 1903

ISADORA UNDER
PLATO'S OLIVE TREE

ISADORA AT COLONUS
PHOTOS: RAYMOND
DUNCAN, GREECE, 1903

GROUND-BREAKING
CEREMONY AT KOPANOS.
TEMPLE DUNCAN,
STANDING BETWEEN
RAYMOND AND ISADORA,
HOLDS THE SHOVEL. TO
ISADORA'S LEFT STAND
SARA, ELIZABETH, AND
DORA DUNCAN

RAYMOND DUNCAN WITH
THE BUILDERS GOING
OVER THE PLANS FOR
KOPANOS
PHOTOS: ATHENS, 1903,
DUNCAN COLLECTION

13 JUN 1903

that when the Norwegian painter Fritz von Thaulow tuned up his fiddle, Isadora agreed to dance. Hampered by her high-waisted Liberty frock and shoes, she simply removed them and danced on the grass in her petticoat. The two young women became close friends.

In the fall, the entire Duncan family was reunited in Berlin. To the dismay of Alexander Grosz, Isadora decided to take a break and do what the family had always dreamed of doing: go to Greece.

Raymond had already decided that all shoes were obnoxious and had begun making his own sandals. Isadora's dancing clothes were starting to influence her street clothes. Now they decided to adopt ancient Greek dress. Augustin reserved Hellenic attire for the stage, Elizabeth and Isadora sometimes wore contemporary dresses and shoes; but Raymond would never again wear modern clothes.

The family, now including Augustin's wife Sarah and their daughter Temple, began the journey from Venice. They traveled to Greece on a fishing boat and continued on foot, then by train, finally arriving in Athens. Their explorations soon led them to a hilltop with an unobstructed view of the Acropolis. They purchased the site for a Duncan family temple and construction began. During the building of "Kopanos," the family camped out on the site, spending alternate nights at the Hotel Angleterre. One

important detail soon came to their attention: there was no water on the hill. Raymond began digging wells, to no avail.

The Greeks were charmed by these eccentric, earnest Americans. Even the King visited their temple. But Isadora and Raymond's time was spent chiefly in research. They were acquainted with Greek drama and poetry; sculpture and vase paintings had given them an image of the dance. But what about the music of the theatre of antiquity? They met the Sikelianos family—Philadelpheus, an archeologist; Angelo, a poet; and Penelope, a musicologist and singer, who became Raymond Duncan's wife.

In the mornings they danced and recited in the ruined Theatre of Dionysus, and in the evenings they went to sit in the moonlight, seeking guidance from the spirits. One night they heard young boys singing old Greek songs: the voices had just the tone needed to reproduce the lost music of the Greek choruses. They selected a group of boys, and with the help of a young seminarian, Panjiotis Tzaanneas, began to train them. On the strength of the theory that many of the hymns of the early Christian

▼
ISADORA DANCING
IN THE THEATRE OF
DIONYSUS
PHOTOS: RAYMOND
DUNCAN, GREECE, 1903

ISADORA WITH
THE CHORUS OF
GREEK BOYS
PHOTO: BERLIN, 1904,
DUNCAN COLLECTION

▼

PROGRAM FROM
ISADORA AND
RAYMOND'S
PRESENTATION OF
THE ANCIENT GREEK
CHORUSES

Church were derived from the strophes and antistrophes of pagan hymns and chants, they searched manuscripts of Byzantine liturgical music to reconstitute the Chorus for Aeschylus' *The Suppliants* and *The Bacchae* of Euripides.

Economic necessity, precipitated by the cost of Kopanos, prompted Isadora's return to Germany, and she took the chorus of boys with her. Dr. Karl Federn, the friend who had translated her pamphlet *The Dance of the Future* into German, was enthusiastic about presenting their musical discovery; but the public in Vienna, Munich, and Berlin preferred Isadora's more approachable work. *The Beautiful Blue Danube*, which had originally been an improvised encore, and which she always found embarrassing in its banality, still brought them to their feet. Also, the Greek boys were growing rapidly, their voices losing the youthful purity that had recommended them. The Duncans sent them back to Athens, and Isadora moved on to another chapter of mythology.

One of Isadora's Munich converts had been Siegfried Wagner, Richard Wagner's son. He had encouraged his mother to invite Isadora to dance at the Festival at Bayreuth. When Cosima Wagner finally decided to issue an invitation in August 1903, Isadora was off to Greece. However, after her return, Isadora received a visit from Cosima and accepted a second invitation to participate in the 1904 Festival.

That summer Isadora took up residence at Phillip's Ruhe, a former imperial hunting lodge. Considering the guest list, it is to her credit that she accomplished any serious work. In addition to her mother and Augustin's daughter Temple, Oscar Beregi visited her, and Mary Desti, with her little son Preston Sturges, both clad in Grecian garments, were living nearby. An endless round of parties began. Cosima Wagner's son-in-law, the art historian Heinrich Thode, fell in love with Isadora. Physically faithful to his wife, he obsessed over Isadora, standing in her moonlit garden, reading to her long into the night, and writing her lengthy, cerebrally passionate letters.

Somewhere above all this social subtext, Isadora found a spiritual space where she could work. Since her arrival in Germany in 1902 she had been studying German, and she was reading philosophy and literature. Karl Federn had introduced her to the works of Kant and Nietzsche. (Is it any wonder that she was attracted to a philosopher who had written, "Let that day be considered lost on which we have not danced"?) From then on, she always kept a copy of Nietzsche's *Thus Spake Zarathustra* with her. Another author whose books she had read with great enthusiasm was Ernst Haeckel, the biologist and philosopher whose *Riddle of the Universe* had become a Darwinian Bible for Isadora. The elderly scientist and the young artist had exchanged touching complimentary letters and photos, and they met that summer.

Haeckel must not have been the only person to enjoy Isadora's performance in spite of its context. She danced the central figure of the Three Graces in the "Bacchanale" in *Tannhäuser*. Her interpretation was based on the composer's own notes calling for, among other qualities, voluptuousness, deliriousness, and, at the end, disorder. Not exactly what one would have expected from the members of the Berlin Ballet. Yet Isadora's fellow Bacchantes were from that ensemble.

Later she would dance her choreography as a solo, and her notes begin:

Alone, today, I can only give you a vague indication, an indefinite sketch of what will later be a multitude of dancers — a mass rushing like a whirlwind in rhythm, caught up by the maddening waves of this music flowing with frenzied and ecstatic sensuality.

Today, we see the "Bacchanale" danced as Wagner and Isadora imagined it.

At this point Isadora decided that she must create a place to welcome the coming dancers of the future — a place in which to nurture the newborn art. She returned to Berlin to found her school.

PENCIL STUDY OF
ISADORA DANCING
BY VALENTINE
LECOMTE, DUNCAN
COLLECTION

PART II

Dramatic: 1903 – 1913

Let us first teach little children to breathe, to vibrate, to feel, and to become one with the general harmony and movement of nature. Let us first produce a beautiful human being, a dancing child. — ISADORA DUNCAN, "MOVEMENT IS LIFE" (1909)

▼▼
THE PRIESTESS,
IPHIGENIA IN TAURIS,
GLUCK
PHOTO: ELVIRA,
MUNICH, CIRCA 1903

Isadora purchased a large house in Grunewald, a residential suburb of Berlin, and furnished it as her first school. In the autumn of 1904 she held auditions in several cities in Germany and chose her first twenty pupils, girls aged six to ten. The children were housed, fed, clothed, and received regular primary education, as well as singing, music, diction, and of course dancing lessons, all free of charge. Elizabeth, who had now taught dance for over a decade, acted as director of the school.

One day in December 1904, Elise de Broukère introduced Edward Gordon Craig to Isadora. Craig, son of the English actress Ellen Terry and the architect and designer Edward William Godwin, was an actor, a designer, a director, and a graphic artist. It is amazing that the two had not met in London, though they knew of each other's work.

Isadora invited Craig to her next recital—a Chopin program, performed in a simple setting designed by Raymond: blue-gray curtains hanging between wooden Greek columns. Craig describes his response:

I shall never forget the first time I saw her come on to an empty platform to dance. Berlin—the year 1904, the month December. Not on a theatre stage was this performance given, but in a concert hall, and you may recall what the platforms were like in 1904.

She came through some little curtains which were not much taller than herself—she came through and walked down to where a musician, his back to us, was seated at a large piano—he had just finished playing a short prelude by Chopin when in she came, and in some five or six steps was standing at the piano, quite still—you might have counted five or eight, and then there sounded the voice of Chopin in a second prelude or étude—it was played through gently

and came to an end—she had not moved at all. Then one step back or sideways, and the music began again as she went moving on before or after it. Only just moving—not pirouetting or doing any of the things which a Taglioni or a Fanny Elssler would have certainly done. She was speaking her own language, not echoing any ballet master, and so she came to move as no one had ever seen anyone move before.

The dance ended, she again stood quite still. No bowing, no smiling—nothing at all. Then again the music is off, and she runs from it—it runs after her then—for she has gone ahead of it.

How is it that we know she is speaking her own language? We know it, for we see her head, her hands, gently active, as are her feet, her whole person. And if she is speaking, what is it she is saying? No one would ever be able to report truly, yet no one present had a moment's doubt.

64

Only this can we say—that she was telling to the air the very things we long to hear; and now we heard them, and this sent us all into an unusual state of joy, and I sat still and speechless.*

Remarkable for its humble and sincere admiration, Craig's memory of Isadora's performance is also particularly interesting for its choice of words. Not only does he describe Isadora's innovative use of music but he refers to her speaking a language, as if she were an actor. When he saw her dance, Craig was not only a man in love with a woman. Of the many artists inspired by Isadora, Craig was perhaps the one who understood and appreciated most deeply what it was that she was doing.

*BBC Radio talk, "Memories of Isadora Duncan"

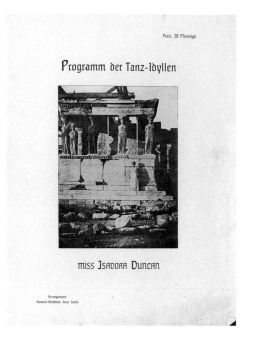

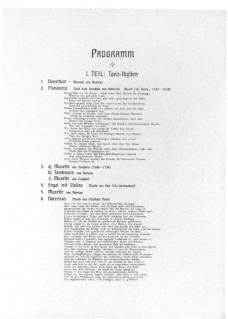

After returning from Greece, Isadora's programs featured Raymond's photo of her standing by the Erectheum. The notice on the third page announced Augustin and Sarah Duncan's recital of scenes from Shakespeare.

Edward Craig wrote later in *Gordon Craig, The Story of this Life* (1968) of his father's reaction:

His silence was induced by a mixture of overwhelming admiration and furious resentment — admiration for what had been to him the greatest artistic experience in his life, resentment that this revelation should come from a woman. Unknown to him, she had been travelling the same path as himself, and it was her unique genius that made it possible for her to show him something about abstract movement which he was still struggling to understand.

Like Isadora, Gordon Craig believed that the theatre must be transformed, that in order to meet the needs of the future, it must return to its ancient function: the expression of the sacred in human society. Craig had left a career as an actor in the Lyceum Theatre company with Henry Irving and Ellen Terry in much the same way that Isadora had left the Daly Company, not from any disenchantment with the theatre, but from the desire to create, to renew the art which was his life's passion.

Recently invented electric lighting was providing possibilities for subtler and more varied effects, and artists were creating three-dimensional scenes to replace the painted backdrops of the Victorian stage. Craig envisioned a theatre where the scene would be an integral, moving part of the performance.

In 1893, Craig learned to make woodcuts. Edward Craig wrote that his father was fascinated by the idea of starting with a black background and slowly introducing light.

This is hardly surprising; it is analogous to the darkened stage gradually being filled with light. For Craig, the work on the drawing table was a prelude to the work on the stage. When critics protested that some of his designs were impossible to realize, he explained that the designs depicted the vision which was to be seen or the emotion which should be felt, not what should be physically placed upon it.

Craig met the organist, composer-conductor Martin Fallas Shaw, in 1897. One day Shaw played Bach's entire *St. Matthew Passion* on the piano, filling in chorus and plot vocally. Craig realized that music could elicit emotion and that emotion could elicit visions from his imagination.

In 1899, Shaw and Craig founded the Purcell Operatic Society, whose aim was the revival of the works of Purcell, Arne, Handel, and Gluck. In May 1900, they produced Purcell's *Dido and Aeneas.* Martin Shaw trained the chorus and orchestra, and Craig created the scenes, costumes, and dances. His notes on these "dances" show that he was choreographing movement to music—not pantomime, where a precut gesture was fitted to a presupposed emotion, but rather symbolic movement. He was striving to create a visual expression, through the movement of the chorus and through the color in the light and scenes; to appeal to the eyes as the music appeals to the ears.

THE HOF-ATELIER
ELVIRA, OWNED BY
SOPHIA GOUDTIKKER,
WAS THE FIRST
WOMEN'S
PHOTOGRAPHIC STUDIO
IN MUNICH. DURING
1903–4 ISADORA WAS
PHOTOGRAPHED THERE
IN POSES FROM HER
DANCES.

"NARCISSUS," CHOPIN
OPUS 64, NO. 2
PHOTOS: ELVIRA,
MUNICH, CIRCA 1903

POLONAISE, CHOPIN
OPUS 40, NO. 1
PHOTOS: ELVIRA,
MUNICH, 1903–4

ORPHEUS, GLUCK
PHOTOS: ELVIRA,
MUNICH, CIRCA 1903

THE PRIESTESS,
IPHIGENIA IN TAURIS,
GLUCK
PHOTOS: ELVIRA,
MUNICH, CIRCA 1903

Their second production, in May 1902, was the London premier of Handel's opera *Acis and Galatea*. With it they presented *The Masque of Love*, a "ballet" of Craig's invention set to Purcell's incidental music for *The Prophetess, or, the History of Dioclesian*. These two productions represented the progression of Craig's concept of a unified stage presentation. He and Shaw had simplified the story of *Dido and Aeneas*, but they went even further with *Acis and Galatea*, giving almost total importance to the music. This freed Craig to pursue simplicity in both the setting and the symbolic movement of the ensemble.

Indeed, Craig's first inspiration for *Dido and Aeneas* had been movement. He had imagined the last scene and had written to Martin Shaw: "One dance I'll make a dance of arms—white *white* arms—The rest of the scene dark—and out of it, the voices—with arm accompaniment." For *Acis and Galatea* and *The Masque of Love*, Craig had devised a very simple notation system dealing with the most natural gestures. He continued to simplify individual gestures in order to heighten the effect produced by the movement of the group, and he concentrated on the progression of movement from one scene to another.

The critics wrote that Craig's work pointed toward a new art and hailed it as "a perfection of beauty." However, the mainstream of British theatre regarded him as a set designer, ignoring the more global theatrical reforms he promulgated.

At this time, Europeans were pursuing theatrical innovation. The Spaniard Mariano Fortuny y Madrazo had invented a domed cyclorama and a system of reflected light that was adopted in many European theatres. He was first and foremost a painter, and he wanted to paint with light. Like Craig, he saw the scene as a moving part of the stage picture, the lighting to be scored like music.

In the summer of 1904, Count Harry Kessler, who took an interest in the court theatre at Weimar, invited Craig to Germany. Dr. Otto Brahm, director of the Lessing Theatre in Berlin, had employed Craig to design the scenes and costumes for Hugo von Hofmannsthal's translation of Thomas Otway's *Venice Preserved*. But Craig did not have the full control he desired and the project ended in a quarrel.

An exhibition of Craig's theatre designs and landscapes opened on December 3 at the Friedmann and Weber Gallery in Berlin. Isadora went to see the work. Craig later wrote:

> *I took her to the door & I can still see her look as the large door closed slowly, she with her eyes on me to the last, I my eyes on her — this moment has often returned to me . . . this farewell after meeting in our particular land.*

On Christmas Day, Isadora arrived in St. Petersburg to dance in the Hall of the Nobles as a benefit for the Society for the Prevention of Cruelty to Children. That winter she was swept into the fantastic twilight of tsarist society and art: carriages full of furs, armloads of fresh flowers, midnight suppers sparkling with champagne and jewels. In her memoirs, Isadora writes of seeing the predawn funeral of the workers who had been shot down in front of the Winter Palace on January 22, 1905, Bloody Sunday. Even then she had an inkling of the importance of this tragedy, for the nascent revolution stirring Russian society was already changing Russian art. The younger dancers longed to experiment and innovate as the actors were doing.

Gordon Craig, left behind in Berlin, began to write love letters to Isadora. In one of the first, he quoted a quatrain from the *Arabian Nights*:

> *She came apparelled in a vest of blue,*
> *That mocked the skies and shamed their azure hue;*
> *I thought thus clad she burst upon my sight,*
> *Like summer moonshine on a wintry night.*

In the audience at Isadora's first performance in Russia—an all-Chopin program—another young man must have experienced much the same emotion. Mikhail Fokine attended with his fellow dancers Anna Pavlova and Tamara Karsavina. The star of the Imperial Ballet, Mathylda Kchessinska, former mistress of the Tsar, had already seen Isadora dance several years earlier in Vienna, and her enthusiasm at Isadora's Russian debut in December 1905, was as great as that of her younger colleagues.

Kchessinska and Pavlova each honored Isadora at supper parties, but Pavlova's must have been the more exciting. The guest list included Serge Diaghilev, who would soon found the Ballets Russes; the painters Alexandre Benois and Léon Bakst; and Vaslav Nijinsky. These progressives of the Russian ballet community were surely well aware of Isadora's work (Imperial Russia being even more a part of Europe than the Soviet society of our recent experience). Their conversation would have been intellectual champagne to rival anything poured by Kchessinska's royal admirers. While Russia's Imperial Ballet represented all that Isadora criticized in contemporary dance, she could not but help admire its strength of technique and respect for the art. It was here that she met young dancers and artists who shared her desire to reform their art. She had reached the epicenter of the dance world.

When Fokine, who had been militating for reform and renewal in dance, saw Isadora embody his dreams, he was galvanized to action. Although they disagreed on the extent to which gymnastics should be used in training and performance, they were more in agreement on the art of dance than many classical and modern dancers of today. Fokine wanted to express emotion; after seeing Isadora, he began to choreograph dances to the music of Chopin, and his use of the head and arms became freer.

His first full-length ballet, *Acis and Galatea*, in "Greek" style, was presented in April 1905 as a graduation performance by the students of the Imperial Ballet School. It met with opposition from the directors, who disapproved of its non-traditional content and form. One of the dancers, remarkable for his agility, was the young Vaslav Nijinsky.

For Fokine, there was no turning back. In February 1907 he presented *Eunice*, drawn from the story *Quo Vadis?* He had studied Greek and Roman art in the Hermitage Museum. He costumed his dancers in tunics, and as bare feet were still too risqué for St. Petersburg, he created the illusion by painting toes on the dancers' tights, which were worn without slippers. That same evening saw the premier of *Chopiniana*. This ballet, now beloved as Les *Sylphides*, is a suite of dances to Aleksandr Glazunov's orchestrations of Chopin piano music, which Isadora had danced since 1900. In the years

to come, Fokine and Pavlova would continue to be influenced by Isadora—in their choice of themes and music, in their choreography, and in their costumes.

Nijinsky later wrote of her:

Isadora has dared to give liberty to movement, enlarged the boundaries in which the artist may evolve and abolished the frontiers established by custom. She has opened the door of their cell to the prisoners. Fokine, the great Fokine, has followed in her footsteps and attained the summit. Before them, in one word, the fantasy and temperament of the dancer were limited.

Meanwhile Craig was designing scenes and costumes for a production of Sophocles' *Elektra* by Eleonora Duse's company; but the production was never mounted. One of the surviving designs shows the extent of Isadora's influence on him at this time: the female figure, clothed in a voluminous white robe, descends a short flight of stairs and gathers the scene around her into her motion. Unlike Craig's previous drawings, in which even the dancers seem suspended in stillness, this woman sweeps forward, emanating light.

At the same time, Craig drew Isadora in her dances. Of the six published in a folio entitled *Isadora Mappe*, only the one drawn from life has the same quality as the *Elektra* design. Craig had accompanied her to Breslau where, on March 2, 1905, she danced at the Thalia Theatre. Standing in the wings, he sketched her dancing to the music of Gluck. On a scrap of paper he wrote in pencil:

At Breslau where she danced more perfectly than ever with more care more freedom more love there they sat still and stupid. How strange a sight. An ugly little theatre full of ugly and foolish people and on the darkened stage a figure growing at each movement more perfect—lavishing beauty on each side of her as a sower sows rich corn in a brown and ugly field—poems glitter and shimmer all round her, floating in the air with her waiting to be flung into the air never to return—all there waiting.

Craig's appraisal of the citizens of Breslau was harsh, as were many of his judgments. Perhaps the little theatre was like the brown field that mutely receives the golden corn; perhaps the audience felt as Craig had felt when he first saw her: awed to stillness. In any case Craig's own stillness had now given way to movement, and his pencils and pens began to dance.

Isadora's next engagements were in Amsterdam and Brussels, and she wrote to Craig that she wished he would go to Greece with her. A few days later, in an undated letter of March 1905, she wrote:

Darling—it's about 3 o'clock—I have been sitting up writing the Marvelous Book! Had a

wonderful torrent of ideas falling over each other. . . . Astounding what I feel when you are not
here . . . twice as sensitive to sounds lights colors etc. Its all a matter of magnetic forces—same
things that keep the earth circling around the sun in constant rhythmetical waves of attraction
and repulsion making the Complete Harmony—Wonderful.

Aren't we wonderful—

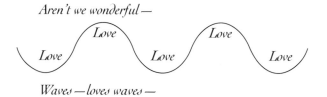

Waves—loves waves—

I've been writing about dance waves sound waves light waves—all the same. . . .
How many thousand miles an hour do light and sound waves travel—so quick travel never-
ceasing love waves from me to you—and from you to me—distance doesn't matter because the
supply is never ceasing. . . .

The "Marvelous Book" was her essay "The Dancer and Nature," published for
the first time in 1928 in *The Art of the Dance*. Sheldon Cheney, the editor of this collection
of Isadora's writings, noted that the essay was "originally written as a dialogue between
two people floating 'in a little bark becalmed' off the shores of Greece; but in a less sentimental moment I. D. or another bluepencilled all but the lines carrying the main

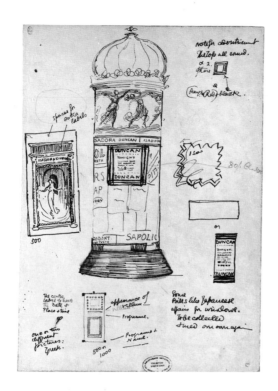

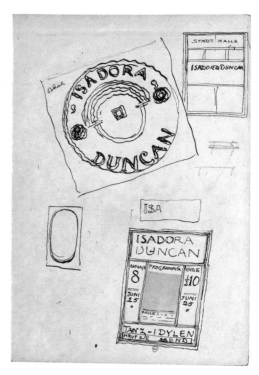

thought. . . ." Alone in a hotel room in Brussels, Isadora longed to be in Greece with Craig, and her love letter became an empowerment to the dancers of the future:

> *One might be led to believe that women are incapable of knowing beauty as an Idea, but I think this only seems so, not because they are incapable of perceiving but only because they are at present blind to the chief means in their power of understanding True Beauty. Through the eyes beauty most readily finds a way to the soul, but there is another way for women—perhaps an easier way—and that is through the knowledge of their own bodies. . . .*
>
> *Not by the thought or contemplation of beauty only, but by the living of it, will women learn. And as form and movement are inseparable, I might say that she will learn by that movement which is in accordance with the beautiful form. . . .*
>
> *. . . Woman is to learn beauty of form and movement through the dance.*
>
> *I believe here is a wonderful undiscovered inheritance for coming womanhood, the old dance which is to become the new. She shall be sculpture not in clay or marble but in her own body which she shall endeavor to bring to the highest state of plastic beauty; she shall be painter, but as part of a great picture, she shall mingle in many groups of new changing light and color. With the movement of her body she shall find the secret of perfect proportion of line and curve. The art of the dance she will hold as a great well-spring of new life for sculpture, painting and architecture. . . .*

Where are we to look for the great fountain-head of movement? Woman is not a thing apart and separate from all other life organic and inorganic. She is but a link in the chain, and her movement must be one with the great movement which runs through the universe; and therefore the fountain-head for the art of the dance will be the study of the movements of Nature.

(Isadora seems such a modern woman that sometimes we forget that she walked around in flowing gowns, capes, and Raymond's handmade sandals among woman constrained by corsets, petticoats, garters, and highbutton shoes. She was speaking to women who had never gone swimming naked, or worn a leotard. Her words, like her dance, were utterly radical in 1905.)

Craig replied to her letter from Brussels: "I'm so glad you've begun your book." He joined her there soon and read what she had written. On his return to Berlin, he wrote to Martin Shaw: "Inspiration is given out by the thousand volt per second from Miss D. And I am alive again (as artist) through her. You know how life-giving or - taking one artist can be to another." On April 22, he began to dictate his own book.

Just two weeks later he had finished *The Art of the Theatre*, written in the form of a dialogue between the Stage Director and the Playgoer. In it Craig set forth his cherished doctrine of the supreme authority of the stage director—the first step toward his complete renewal of the theatre through unity of taste and purpose. Maurice Magnus translated it into German, Count Kessler wrote a preface, and it was published that summer as *Die Kunst des Theaters*.

In one of Isadora's notebooks there is a draft of an amusing review of *Die Kunst des Theaters*. She hails Craig as "Mr. Vesuvius Theatre Destroyer" creating "C L E A R S P A C E ," and invites him to "Step up now and show us—what's to happen next." An English edition of the book was being prepared, and in the same notebook are her ideas for possible expansion. They reflect the hope that Isadora never lost for the performing artist as creator:

This pamphlet is a sketch or part of a large book entitled The Art of the Theatre, in which I intend to write chapters on: the scene painter, the costume maker, the actor, the lights, the play, the author, the chorus, the dancer, the action, the gesture, the words, the word inflection, and all these things in their relation to the theatre and in relation to each other and expressing themselves as one.

What the theatre should be:

The brain and heart of the nation. The reflection point of the nation's highest intellect. The constant mirror of its noble strivings toward the highest beauty. What was the theatre once? A coming together of thought in its highest form. Action, music and dance.

Isadora was speaking of women and men as the center of the new theatre, but Craig was already thinking in the opposite direction—toward the distillation and abstraction of human activity and presence on stage. Foreshadowed in *The Art of the Theatre* is the concept of the perfect, passionless interpreter, who would be completely controlled by the stage director: the Ubermarionette. Craig was considering the possibility of marionettes—and their superiority over poor human creatures governed by passion—and he asked Isadora to shop for wooden marionettes while she was in Brussels. Although their eyes would be on each other to the last, Isadora and Craig were already turning their steps toward the opposite frontiers of what he had called their "own particular land."

On July 20, 1905, Isadora danced at Kroll's Opera House in Berlin. On stage with

her were her pupils, and the performance was a great success—her school was a reality. In October the children danced again, this time alone, at the Theater des Westens. Elizabeth then took them on a tour through Germany. Isadora had not intended them to dance in public so soon, but financial considerations made it hard to ignore their success.

In spite of her full touring schedule, Isadora continued to explore new choreographic possibilities, among them the notion of dance without music. One of Craig's letters refers to Isadora's "musicless movements" and inquires about her progress, but her reply gently reminded him that it was difficult to work in a railway carriage. He was now acting as her business manager and her bookings included many one-night engagements.

For Christmas 1905, Isadora received what she wanted more than anything: the assurance that she was pregnant.

Dearest Heart

. . . The Dr. was here this morning, he says I must be careful but that I can dance till end of May—I wish you would know that in all the hundreds of times you have kissed me there hasn't been one that everything in me hasn't cried out—make me fruitful—give me a child. . . . I can't help feeling happy about it . . . but that's no good to you—

I wish you would send someone to Sweden—I am sure Sweden in the month of April would be as good as Holland—and cover the summer—Dr. says I can probably dance again next Dec. 1—Listen, that isn't so bad—Love to you—

Your Isadora

Craig was already the father of many children—four children by his wife, one by his mistress, and three by his life-long companion Elena Meo (more would follow in the years to come, by other women). Elena's last child, their son Teddy (Edward Craig), had been born in January 1905, only a few weeks after he met Isadora.

Early in 1906 Isadora set off on tour with Craig, to earn enough money to "cover the summer." In March, Martin Shaw joined them. Isadora was dancing mostly to Gluck and Schubert, generally with a different orchestra at each performance, so Shaw's collaboration was invaluable to her.

The evening of Shaw's arrival in Berlin, Craig took him directly from the station to the theatre. Shaw describes the scene:

That evening . . . It was her Gluck programme. I had never seen her before and the simplicity and beauty of her movements gave me deep enjoyment. There were no leaps or pirouettes, only beautiful floating movements and gestures. The theatre was crowded and the audience in a state of ecstatic delight throughout. Isadora provided the whole programme. This in itself was remarkable.

. . . Craig's decors were just right and seemed part of the dance. After the performance I was taken round to see the wonderful creature in her dressing room. . . . All her movements were deliberate, reposeful, never for an instant hurried or nervous. One simply could not imagine her catching a train.

. . . Her serenity made me think of a still, deep lake over which no breeze made the faintest ripple.

This was a time of artistic triumph and personal joy for Isadora, but public opinion about her private life began to create new difficulties. Elizabeth Duncan had organized a committee of wealthy, influential patrons for the Duncan School. Some of them had been shocked by the children dancing bare-legged in public; more were now shocked by the news that Isadora was pregnant with Craig's child. Others remained loyal in their support, but the loss of patronage would increase her burden in maintaining the school and paying its staff.

In June, Isadora retired to the Villa Maria on the North Sea at Noordwijk in Holland. There, by the waves she so loved, she awaited the birth of her child. From

Grunewald her little niece Temple came to visit her and inspired Isadora to write the essay "A Child Dancing":

> The child must not be taught to make movements, but her soul, as it grows to maturity must be guided and instructed; in other words, the body must be taught to express itself by means of the motions which are natural to it. . . . These first memoranda in my notebook come back to my memory as I sit here watching Temple dancing on the beach. Her dancing is, in a sense, an epitome of all the hopes and all the efforts I have expended on my school since its foundation.

Isadora sent for her friend Kathleen Bruce. The birth was an extremely difficult one, and Kathleen's support was a comfort. Craig was present when, on September 24, their daughter was born. Isadora stayed on a while to recover before returning to Berlin.

The introduction to Craig's folio *Isadora Mappe* was in the form of a poem. It ended:

I see Calmness and Beauty both the Strong and the Sweet

advancing now with perfect ease

All makes way for this spirit

Nothing can hinder it.

Three marks of a pencil, or three hundred

it is ever the same Picture

A note sounded, or a fall of notes,

It is the same Dance.

Something put down

a Record

Something uttered on that divine theme understood

so easily, and only with ease

that theme which commences

"I AM HAPPY. . . ."

and which ends in

". . . it is Beautiful"

This is the theme she dances

Not yet has she depicted a Gloom or a Sorrow unbearable

For ever it seems Sunlight with her

The little Shadows themselves are found out

and move away as she passes

This is the great power

She comes of the lovely family

The great Companions

That Conquering Race which has held up the

World so that it might spin without difficulty.

The courageous Giants

the Preservers of Beauty

the Answerers of all Riddles.

That winter, at the home of their mutual friends Giulietta and Robert von Mendelssohn, Isadora and Craig met the great Italian tragedian Eleonora Duse. Years before, as a young actor in London, Craig had gone to her dressing room to offer his congratulations, but this was their first social meeting. Duse had been impressed with his designs for *Elektra* (the project was dropped only because it would have been too

difficult to take on tour), and she asked him to do scenery for a production of Ibsen's
Rosmersholm.

Craig had recently refused an offer from Max Reinhardt because it did not give
him full control, but Isadora urged him to accept Duse's commission. It would afford
Europe its first glimpse of Craig's vision of the "spiritual territory" he thought the stage
should be.

With her baby at her breast, Isadora accompanied Craig to Florence. There she
kept Duse company while Craig painted a vast blue and green backdrop to replace the
bourgeois salon of the author's directions. As Duse spoke no English and Craig no
French or Italian, Isadora interpreted. She did not literally translate their conversations;
if she had, the project would never have gotten past the Mendelssohns' front door.
But her instinct was correct. Not only was Duse pleased with Craig's work, she understood it.

Rosmersholm was performed only once, on the evening of December 5, 1907, at the Teatro alla Pergola. Craig wrote to Martin Shaw:

> *It was a success & is—Duse was magnificent—.... She says "I'll never have any other scenes."... Is it not happiness to find this still alive in the theatres.... The pleasure I got from seeing Miss Duncan watching my work with Duse was infinite....*

And he wrote somewhat prophetically to his mother:

> *Duse said ... it is the same with plays as with people, one does not love the same person and one cannot always love the same play, but to renew love—that is the secret, not to hang on to past & dead things—to sweep all past away & to continually renew....*

Isadora returned to work. She had sent her mother with the baby and her nurse, Marie Kist, to San Remo. From the Hotel Bristol in Warsaw she wrote to Craig of uprisings, broken contracts, toothaches, food poisoning, and more. But in spite of it all, her thoughts were centered on her work:

Dearest—I slipped into my old dresses & my old dances last night like a charm. After rehearsing the orchestra all day—& great agony of spirit—suddenly felt myself dancing like a miracle.... The town looks sad enough here—& I am glad if my dance can bring to some people here a little joy....

I found something quite new for me this afternoon—only a little movement but something I have never done before & may be the key note to a great deal.... I need help with it....

... I feel so dissatisfied with my work & that infernal Blue Danube....

I work some each day. Something is on the way but comes slowly. Its a music question. I must settle once and for all—antique? Early Italian? Gluck? Modern? or None?...

But I've found one new movement which I think will astonish you....

—DECEMBER 18, 1906

Isadora's Christmas card enclosed another letter:

Darling—Just came home from dancing—Chopin on orchestra is such a success that it frightens me! Schubert falls quite flat afterward.... I feel something dimly coming—I badly

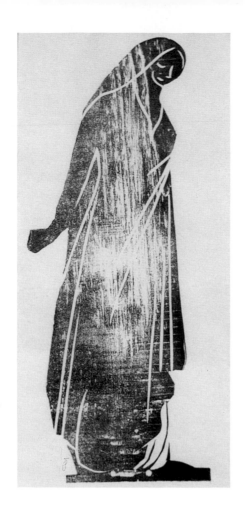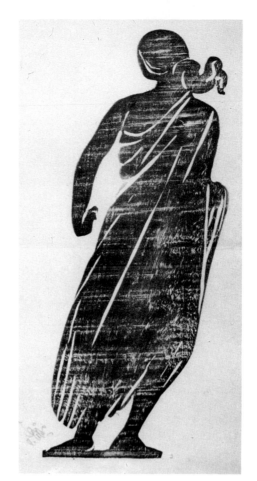

need a musician to help me. . . . I would like someone to help me learn more about music, and study exactly its different relations to dancing. . . . I heard the Pathétique Symphonie of Tchaikowski — Wonderful — Go & hear it when you have a chance. Tell me what you think: does the dance spring from the music, or should the music accompany the dance — or should they both be born together.

Martin Shaw joined her again in Holland in late January 1907 to conduct for her. She continued to tour and work on new dances until she collapsed from illness brought on by exhaustion and the effects of her recent difficult childbirth. Craig visited her and then returned to Berlin, where he received a telegram from Duse.

Initially, Duse had agreed with the grand scale of Craig's ideas. But when she presented *Rosmersholm* in Nice in February, the stage manager of the Casino Theatre found the backdrop too high for the proscenium, so he amputated the lower three feet. This solved his problem, but ruined the proportions of the scene. When Craig arrived, he was enraged. Not even Isadora's diplomacy could avert a rupture. Duse had expressed the hope of working further with Craig, but now she was put off by his lack of self-control.

Isadora collapsed again and had to spend some time in Nice recuperating. Craig fled the tense and unhappy situation. In the South of France, at Vence (where he would spend his last years), he made his first copperplate etching. From there he traveled on to Florence to join Martin Shaw, who was searching for new music for Isadora.

When Craig left Isadora in Nice, they must have known that the parting was definitive, for their letters refer to Elena and their children joining him in Italy. But Isadora hoped that working together would keep them close.

The summer of 1907 was tiring and fruitless for Isadora. Craig was still nominally her business manager, although Augustin was now actually doing that work. Still, Isadora agreed to send Craig money to pay for his projects—the building of his model theatre, his etchings, and his publication, *The Mask*. Bookings were fewer than expected and managers difficult, resulting in little income, but she sent what she could and satisfied the bailiffs, who had attached the contents of his Berlin studio. Craig, who was not earning anything at the moment, replied with recriminations.

In December, Isadora returned to Russia. In her Moscow audience was Konstantin Stanislavsky, director of the Moscow Art Theatre. He had first seen her dance in 1905, but had not met her until now. When she was not dancing, Isadora attended his plays. Stanislavsky was working on his system for actors and the members of his company, and his students participated in the research. When he spoke with Isadora, he realized why her art touched him so deeply. He wrote later:

> *From that time on I never missed a single one of Duncan's concerts. The necessity to see her often was dictated from within me by an artistic feeling that was closely related to her art. Later, when I became acquainted with her methods as well as the ideas of her great friend Gordon Craig, I came to know that in different corners of the world, due to conditions unknown to us, various people in various spheres sought in art for the same naturally born creative principles. Upon meeting they were amazed at the common character of their ideas. This is exactly what happened at the meeting I am describing. We understood each other almost before we had said a single word. . . she came to our theatre and I received her as a guest of honor. This reception became general, for our entire company joined me, as they had all come to know and love her as an artist.*

Stanislavsky tells of Isadora speaking about her need to place the creative motor in her soul, before setting foot on the stage. This was precisely what Stanislavsky be-

lieved an actor must do. They agreed that the artist must first feel emotionally what he or she is to convey physically; that gesture and utterance must spring from within, not be dictated from without.

Isadora immediately suggested that Stanislavsky bring Craig to Moscow. Since Stanislavsky had superhuman patience, and a faithful and dedicated company, the collaboration resulted in the most complete production Craig would ever mount. As Craig put it, Stanislavsky was able to leave his "common sense in the cloak room" and rely on his "finer senses." The Moscow Art Theatre production of *Hamlet* finally opened on January 8, 1912. Craig's movable screens—the first, and only physically realized version of his moving scene concept—were difficult to manipulate with traditional stage machinery, but they paved the way for non-representational stage scenery.

In the transcripts of the two men's conversations about the play, Isadora's name appears on several occasions. Craig had always seen himself as Hamlet and Isadora

now became Ophelia. One day Stanislavsky asked Craig whether he knew of an actress capable of the stillness they desired in Ophelia's movement. Stanislavsky suggested Duse. Craig replied firmly: no!

S: *I know of only one, but she does not like to speak.*

C: *Who is that?*

S: *Duncan.*

C: *Oh no! she cannot.*

It seems as if the mention of her name revealed Craig's innermost thoughts. In his own copy of the play, Craig wrote her initials five times in the margin of Act III, scene i, where Hamlet speaks to Ophelia.

Ham.:   *Ha, Ha! Are you honest!*

Oph.:   *My Lord?*

Ham.:   *Are you fair?*

Oph.:   *What means your lordship?*

Ham.:   *That if you be honest and fair, your honesty should admit no discourse to your beauty.*

Oph.:   *Could beauty, my lord, have better commerce than with honesty?*

Ham.:   *Ay, truly; for the power of beauty will sooner transform honesty from what it is to a bawd than the force of honesty can translate beauty into his likeness. This is sometimes a paradox, but now the time gives it proof. I did love you once.*

Oph.:   *Indeed, my lord, you made me believe so.*

Ham.:   *You should not have believ'd me, for virtue cannot so inoculate our old stock but we shall relish of it. I loved you not.*

Oph.:   *I was the more deceived.*

Craig underlined Hamlet's farewells to Ophelia and noted:

these farewells are cried from a distance, further, further, further—although he is close here....

This scene is love, love, love—over & over again—no fury—no anger—nothing but love in agony.

In the years between 1908 and 1912 much changed in Isadora's life. In March 1908, she and Craig, together briefly in Berlin, agreed to name their daughter (whom they had called only Baby or Snowdrop) Deirdre. Craig always said how Irish Isadora was and it seemed appropriate that their little girl's name should mean "beloved of Ireland."

Isadora had become Auguste Rodin's neighbor; she was renting a studio in the as yet unrestored Hôtel Biron (today the Rodin Museum). Among other artists who lived

ELIZABETH WITH
(*L. TO R.*): MARGOT,
MARIA, ANNA,
AND IRMA

LISA AND TEMPLE
DANCING

ANNA AND IRMA
DANCING
PHOTOS: PAUL BERGER,
PARIS, 1908

and worked there were Henri Matisse, Jean Cocteau, the sculptor Clara Westhoff, and her husband the poet Rainer Maria Rilke.

On the second of her two Russian tours in 1908, Isadora was accompanied by her students. She had taught them the chorus dances from Gluck's *Iphigenia in Aulis* and they created a sensation. There was serious discussion of establishing Isadora's school there. Stanislavsky wanted it to be a part of the Moscow Art Theatre School, but financially he could not support it. Kchessinska readily acknowledged Isadora's influence on the ballet, and was impressed by her students, but of course the two dancers disagreed on the fundamental basis of their art. However, the ballerina did not offer any formal opposition, and the budget of the Imperial Theatres could easily have accommodated the relatively modest cost of the Duncan School.

The real opposition came from musicians. Nikolai Rimsky-Korsakov stated that "what repels me . . . is that she foists her art upon and tacks it onto musical composi-

95 DRAMATIC: 1903–1913

ISADORA'S BEETHOVEN
PROGRAM, WHICH
INCLUDED THE SEVENTH
SYMPHONY, WAS
CONTROVERSIAL. THE
COMPOSITION WAGNER
HAD CALLED "THE
APOTHEOSIS OF THE
DANCE" WAS
CONSIDERED BY SOME
TO BE TOO SACRED FOR
CHOREOGRAPHIC
INTERPRETATION.

tions . . . whose authors do not at all need her company, and have not reckoned with it." He was not alone in this feeling that Isadora was disrespectful in dancing, for instance, Beethoven's Seventh Symphony. What could she possibly add to a masterpiece? Was her dancing not a distraction? How could she claim to interpret the work of a long-dead master? Today, no one questions a dancer's right to use the finest music, even if it was not originally composed for dance. And indeed during her lifetime, many of the finest musicians, conductors, and composers worked happily with Isadora. Still more praised her contribution to their art.

In June 1908 she went to London with her students. To her great joy, she at last met Craig's mother, Ellen Terry, and wrote to him that "She was like a great lovely Goddess Angel to me — & the two nights she came to the theatre I danced as in a dream — I was so excited at her being there. . . ." The feeling was mutual. Ellen Terry rose to her feet and cried out to the rest of the audience: "Do you realize what you are looking at? Do you understand that this is the most incomparably beautiful dancing in the world?" The critics agreed: "We have never seen an art so joyous, so purely beautiful as that of Isadora Duncan. . . . We have never seen such a joy of life as we saw in these children. . . ."

Another American, Ruth St. Denis, first saw her compatriot at the Duke of York's Theatre that summer:

> It is difficult to find words with which to pay tribute to the indescribable genius of Isadora. I can only say briefly that she evoked in that pitifully small audience visions of the morning of the world. She had not only the spirit of Greece in her effortless, exquisitely modulated rhythms but she was the whole human race moving in that joy and simplicity and childlike harmony that we associate with Fra Angelico's angels dancing "the dance of the redeemed." Mary Fanton Roberts said years afterwards that "Isadora was Dionysiac and Ruth St. Denis Apollon," meaning that Isadora possessed the ecstatic liberation of the soul, which I translated into form, and it was some of this ecstatic quality of her soul that I received on this occasion, never to lose as long as I live. In one arm's movement was all the grace of the world, in one backward flying of the head was all nobility.

Ruth St. Denis's mention of the pitifully small audience reminds us that while most of her fellow artists and the critics were enchanted by Isadora, and she touched a great number of the general public, there were still many people who preferred to be "entertained." Her competition in Paris had been Diaghilev's season of Russian concerts at the Opera. These had great artistic merit, of course, but they also had behind them

the full force of his genius as an impresario, and they were social events as well.

In London, her competition was of a lower order. Maud Allen, another Californian, who imitated Isadora, was performing her *Salomé* dance at the Palace Theatre vaudeville. Although the same critics who praised Isadora called Allen's a "repulsive performance, and one which we should not consent on any account to witness a second time," many of the people who preferred to be entertained enjoyed watching Allen drop those seven veils.

Martin Shaw wrote later, in 1929, that when Isadora danced in London, the response was "what one would have expected. I am almost inclined to think that the possible reason for this is that there was no sex appeal in Isadora's dancing. That in itself was new and strange, and the English public does not like anything new or strange." Isadora would have taken his opinion as a compliment. The idea of the naughty-but-nice dancing girl on the "wicked stage," imported from England, was just what she, and Ruth St. Denis, had fought against years before in America.

But the fact remained that for Isadora, commercial success was a necessity as the

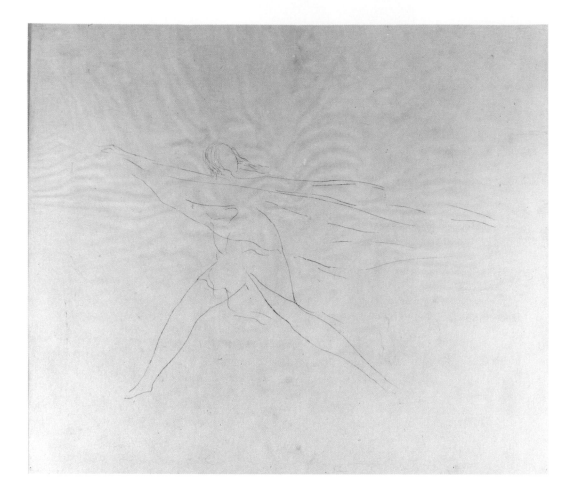

cost of running her school was enormous. Later, in 1908, she accepted an offer to tour in the United States. Charles Frohman mistook her *Iphigenia* for a Broadway attraction and engaged a second-rate orchestra. He then decided that her work was over the heads of the American public. After terminating the contract, Isadora stayed on a while in New York, her discouragement mitigated by the enthusiasm of the artistic community. The sculptor George Grey Barnard wanted her to pose for a monumental statue to be entitled "American Dancing," which was never completed. She met American artists who had not yet seen her, owing to the long time she had spent in Europe. Among them were the painters and sculptors Arthur B. Davies, George Bellows, Robert Henri, Van Deering Perrine, Ruth Reeves, John Sloan, and Lorado Taft; the writers and poets Max Eastman, Percy MacKaye, William Vaughn Moody, Edwin Arlington Robinson, and Ridgely Torrence; and the conductor Walter Damrosch.

Damrosch proposed a collaboration. In November, Isadora was dancing

101 DRAMATIC: 1903–1913

Beethoven's Seventh Symphony and the music of Chopin with the New York Symphony Orchestra, at the Metropolitan Opera House. As in Russia there were critics and musicians who disagreed with her dancing such music, while others recognized her remarkable musicality. One critic wrote that

> *Her appeal was as much to the mind as to the eye. She develops a theme as consistently as the composer she chooses to interpret. As the themes of Beethoven's Allegretto came and went they were caught into a new synthesis by the recurring movements and paces of the dancer. . . . The relations between the counterpoint and the figures of the dance were most lucid. Not only did they interpret. They translated.*

In a way, Isadora had rendered her body a musical instrument; she had become a member of the orchestra. She herself wrote:

> *Often I thought to myself, what a mistake to call me a dancer—I am the magnetic center to convey the emotional expression of the orchestra.*

Seen in its proper context, her work delighted American audiences. President Theodore Roosevelt attended her Washington performance. After their success, Duncan and Damrosch signed a contract for five months of the following year—1909—before Isadora returned to Paris to fulfill an engagement at the Trocadero.

Due to the U. S. child labor laws, Isadora would not have been able to present the children on stage in New York, so she had left them in France with Elizabeth. Max Merz, who had begun his career as a rehearsal pianist at Grunewald, was distraught at the idea of the school being moved from Germany and had convinced Elizabeth that they should form their own school, independent of Isadora. Elizabeth began to work on this project. Soon the Grand Duke of Hesse granted her property at Darmstadt for her new school.

Upon returning to Paris, Isadora rented two large apartments, one for herself and one for her pupils, but it was evident that even with her recent successes she would not be able to reestablish her school in France. She had begun, in jest at first, to say, "I must find a millionaire!" She was dancing again at the Gâité-Lyrique. Lugné-Poe, director of the Théâtre de L'Oeuvre, acting as her artistic director, had engaged Edouard Colonne and

his orchestra. Her pupils were once again appearing with her in the *Iphigenia*, and one day the millionaire attended their performance.

Paris Singer, heir to the Singer sewing-machine fortune, was the brother of the Princesse de Polignac. He fell passionately in love with Isadora.

Isadora had decided that during the summer the twelve girls should spend some time with their own families, so she sent them all home. Now Max Merz lost no time in contacting their families to let them know that Elizabeth's school was ready to receive them. Since they were all German, with the exception of one Swiss child, this must have seemed preferable to Isadora's plan to relocate the school in France.

By this time Isadora had become an icon for artists, especially in Paris. Many had first seen her in 1903, when she and Raymond had gone to the Ecole des Beaux-Arts and distributed complimentary tickets to the students, and they had never missed a performance since. Her image followed them back to their studios. The painter and engraver

André Dunoyer de Segonzac published his first Isadora portfolio in 1910, with a preface in verse by the poet Fernand Divoire. The same year Jean-Paul Lafitte published his studies with a preface by the art historian Elie Faure. José Clara and Jules Grandjouan were working on drawings which would contribute to their portfolios. Valentine Lecomte, who had begun sketching Isadora in 1903, continued to record her dances. Lecomte's work covers the entire span of Isadora's career and shows the changes in her art—from lyrical to dramatic and later, tragic.

In the United States, Abraham Walkowitz sketched her continuously from 1908. Even after her death he would return to her image in sketches that reflected his own changing style. There are no films of Isadora dancing, so Walkowitz's drawings are the closest we have to a moving image of Isadora. Viewed in succession, these deceptively simple line drawings convey the great muscular strength, the unusual suppleness, and the infinite subtle variety of her movements.

The sculptor Emile-Antoine Bourdelle had met Isadora in 1903 at Rodin's picnic, but it was in 1909 that he first saw her dance on stage. The nymph who had been persuaded to take off her skirt and dance on the grass in her muslin petticoat had grown into the beautiful, tragic muse. Bourdelle had already been asked to decorate the facade of the planned Théâtre des Champs-Elysées. When he saw Isadora, he realized that she was his muse: "To me it seemed that there, through her, was animated an ineffable frieze wherein divine frescoes slowly became human realities. Each leap, each attitude

Isadora, bending and
throwing back her
fine head, closes her
eyes to dance within
her pure emotion. . . .
All my muses in the
theatre are
movements seized
during Isadora's
flight; she was my
principle source.
—Emile-Antoine
Bourdelle

of the great artist remains in my memory like flashes of lightning." Bourdelle would return from the theatre and sketch for hours. His images of Isadora are the most varied, for they convey not only Isadora but the vast range of emotions she embodied.

Work on the theatre progressed rapidly. Having seen Isadora and Nijinsky dance together at a party in Paris during the Ballets Russes season, Bourdelle decided to include masculine figures in his frieze. *The Dance* portrays Isadora and Nijinsky together; *The Tragedy*, Iphigenia and the High Priest. In *The Meditation of Apollo, the Muses run toward Apollo,* all of the Nine Muses are Isadora in her different aspects.

The interior of the theatre is also dedicated to the image of Isadora. Maurice Denis painted four great murals of women in her image and a bas-relief of dancing children. Even the curtain in the adjoining small theatre, by Roussel, depicts a *Fête Dionysiac.* The Théâtre des Champs-Elysées opened its doors on April 2, 1913, one of the last happy days of Isadora's life; it remains the most tangible monument to her art and her spirit.

But while Bourdelle was creating his masterpiece, Isadora relaxed a little. Paris Singer gloried in dressing her as befitted her beauty and fame. It was probably on a visit to Venice that she acquired the first of many Delphos dresses. Mariano Fortuny's elegant pleated silk creation had the classic simplicity of her own dancing dresses; and she ordered a miniature for Deirdre. In Paris, Paul Poiret was dressing women in art. When Isadora began to advocate dress reform, she had been among the few pioneers

who convinced a handful of women to adopt their minimalist attire. Now Poiret offered the comfort of clothing with very simple lines, following the body, and the excitement of the most fantastic designs and exotic fabrics. Isadora was one of many theatre artists who delighted in his creations, along with women for whom they were a total novelty.

Isadora could entertain on the most lavish scale. Instead of simple soirées in a barren studio attended by fellow artists, she gave remarkable parties. Even before she met Singer, she had purchased the former studio of the muralist Henri Gervex in Neuilly, and Poiret decorated it for her. Her plain blue curtains remained in the studio, but there were mysterious corners of black and gold elsewhere. One summer evening Isadora and Singer gave a party at the Trianon Palace Hotel in Versailles. The Colonne Orchestra played Gluck and Wagner for the guests, who included all the artistic and political luminaries of Paris. The aging Rodin sent a note, addressed to "Dear & great Artist," saying he didn't want to get home too late, but that he would come for the music. It rained during dinner, but after the storm had passed the garden was illuminated and Isadora danced for her guests.

Perhaps, like some of Isadora's other friends, Rodin felt nostalgic for the empty

studio with its plain blue curtains. Stanislavsky, on a visit to Paris, wrote of feeling uneasy lunching with Isadora and Singer in a fashionable restaurant. Singer was genuinely interested in her art, but like any civilian who has dined with a table full of theatre people he must have wondered sometimes how they could tirelessly discuss Shakespeare or Gluck for hours on end. This was to be a source of tension throughout their relationship, along with the fact that Singer wanted Isadora to marry him and she did not want to marry anyone.

In September 1909, Isadora learned that she was pregnant again. Nonetheless, she left for America and another successful tour with Walter Damrosch. The fact that Isadora continued to dance joyously, proud of her approaching motherhood, shocked many American ladies. Of course Miss Duncan explained that she was celebrating life, but they felt it should be done a bit more privately. In any case she found it physically prudent to give a last performance on December 2, 1909, at Carnegie Hall.

During Isadora's rise to international fame, her brother Augustin had become a respected actor and director, leaving New York only between roles to work on projects with Isadora. Raymond, whom Martin Shaw remarked was "also a wonderful dancer,"

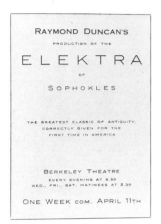

RAYMOND DUNCAN'S

PRODUCTION OF THE

ELEKTRA

OF

SOPHOKLES

THE GREATEST CLASSIC OF ANTIQUITY,
CORRECTLY GIVEN FOR THE
FIRST TIME IN AMERICA

BERKELEY THEATRE

EVERY EVENING AT 8.30
WED., FRI., SAT. MATINEES AT 2.30

ONE WEEK COM. APRIL 11TH

THE ELEKTRA
OF
SOPHOKLES

CAST

Klytaimnestra	Eleni Sikelianos
	(of the Royal Theatre, Athens, Greece)
Orestis	Dionysos Devaris
	(of the New Theatre Athens, Greece)
Pedagogos	Andrea Devaris
Aigisthos	Raymond Duncan
Chrysothemis	Iola Palaiologos
First semi-chorus	Gerasimus Soumilas
Second semi-chorus	Demetrius Phatouros
The lyric chorus dances	RAYMOND DUNCAN
and	
ELEKTRA	PENELOPE DUNCAN

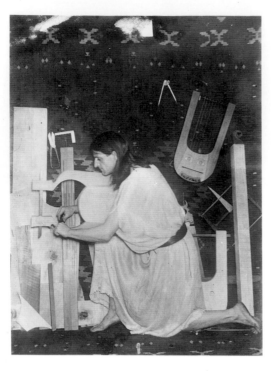

had been working, as usual, on a variety of projects. He and Penelope were at Kopanos, where they had begun a utopian colony living an entirely natural existence, raising goats for the hair and milk, and spinning and weaving their own clothing. In 1908 they were in Berlin, printing Raymond's book of woodcuts of Hellenic vase paintings when he completed the designs for his ideal type. (Raymond had been a printer in his youth in San Francisco, and longed to reform typography as his sister was reforming dance.) He had the sans-serif letters carved in wood in London in 1909 and later made his own metal type. But for Raymond—as for Isadora and Augustin—the theatre was central to his life.

Raymond had researched ancient Greek music with Penelope, and he had devised a system of gymnastics, used to strengthen the body for dance and everyday movements. His exhaustive studies of Greek vase paintings furnished him with forms and movements to emulate. They then embarked on full productions. By 1910, their company was ready to tour the United States. Sponsored by Hellenic societies across the country, they presented Sophocles' *Elektra* in Greek, with accompanying music and dance. It was an historic event in the American theatre, though one that appealed to a very select audience.

On their return to Paris they performed at the Châtelet, and it was while sharing

the theatre for rehearsals that Nijinsky saw Raymond's company dancing in profile, like a frieze come alive. The movements of the Greek Chorus in his ballet *Afternoon of a Faun*, so often said to be inspired by Isadora, were in fact inspired by Raymond's dance movement. It was decidedly more stylized than Isadora's, Apollonian rather than Dionysian, and performed to the music of re-creations of Greek instruments.

Raymond and Penelope decided to stay on in Paris and establish their own school, the Akademia Duncan. Raymond would soon open a theatre there, to present his own work and that of anyone whose message he thought worth promoting.

Singer had renamed his yacht *Isis*—the Egyptian goddess of fertility, and his pet name for Isadora. After a cruise up the Nile they went to his villa at Beaulieu, where on May 1, 1910, Patrick Augustus Duncan was born. This birth was easy and Isadora was soon at work once again. During the summer, they went back to Singer's estate in Devonshire; she completed her Gluck choreography and worked on Wagner.

She was dancing the "Bacchanale" from *Tannhäuser*, the "Flower Maidens" from *Parsifal*, and the "Liebestod" from *Tristan und Isölde*. Her art had ripened, and she was a mature woman expressing the full range of emotions she had experienced. The dances for Gluck's *Orpheus* were remarkable in their scope. Isadora played one of the Blessed Spirits in the Elysian Fields but also the Furies in Hades. Her portrayal of the damned

and demonic Furies was unlike any dance seen on stage before. Sweeping the stage with her hair, clawing the air with contorted fingers, mouthing unutterable screams, vainly writhing in hideously reptilian postures, she was repulsive to behold, the personification of impotent evil. This was dance at its ugliest—a terrifying portrayal of the dark side of soul. This was Modern Dance, unafraid of the reality. Even the once uncertain American audiences appreciated her work.

To this period also belongs the lush, romantic suite of waltzes to the music of Brahms—coy, flirtatious, sensual, a woman dancing for her lover. And indeed she was loved. Singer was waiting eagerly for her to return from this tour, which lasted from February to April 1911. So were her dear children.

Deirdre wrote to her in French, with very good penmanship:

Dear Mama

We are well. When are you coming home? Patrick is playing music. I had a good time at the circus. I know how to read and write now.

I kiss you.

Deirdre

and she helped Patrick to print a postscript:

Mama, I kiss you.

When the loving mother returned home in April, her darling Patrick ran to meet her. He had learned to walk; soon he would be dancing.

Singer greeted her with a plan. For some time he had shared her concern about her original pupils, who had now been at Elizabeth's school for over two years. What their parents—and Isadora—had not known when they went to join the new school was that Max Merz believed in the ideal of "racial purity" and was more interested in producing joyful specimens of German womanhood than dancers. The girls whom Fernand Divoire had christened "the Isadorables" were being subjected to *Korperkultur* gymnastic training, and their silk tunics had been replaced by scratchy gray woolen ones.

Isadora and Singer knew that the school must be established in France. To this end Singer had purchased a piece of property on the rue de Berri, near the Champs-Elysées.

The architect Louis Sue drew up plans for a theatre in which Isadora could perform with her students, to show her art in its complete form. Isadora suggested that Craig might design the lighting and scenery, but of course the fact that it was "Miss Duncan's theatre," designed by Mr. Sue, and that the money was Mr. Singer's, made the association impossible for him.

The Princesse de Polignac was interested in forming a permanent orchestra, and there was a suggestion of eliminating the boxes to leave room for a large standing-room

section for students and artists. One of Singer's letters mentions his amusing agreement with this idea:

> *I have been living in the theatre for some weeks and I know my way about it with my eyes shut. The more I think of it the less I care for the idea of having boxes since they would be right at the back of the theatre in the very heart of your enthusiasm and unlike Bayreuth would be occupied by the people least likely to be enthusiastic — "the over-fed rich." If I were you I should either continue the cheap seats there or have a standing promenade as suggested by Mme. Buletaud.*

Isadora and Augustin had been working on plans for full productions of Greek tragedies. They had chosen Gilbert Murray's translations of the plays of Euripides and discussed the idea of new music with Walter Damrosch. She hoped that her students would have the privilege of sharing the stage with Mounet-Sully and Duse. The neighbors however objected to having a theatre on their street, and for lack of a building permit the project was shelved.

Isadora was concentrating harder than ever on her work. In January 1913 she left

for Russia with the pianist Hener Skene. She missed Deirdre and Patrick dreadfully and sent for them to meet her in Berlin, where she was performing on her way home. She had been having strange premonitions. One night, in mid-performance, she asked Skene to play Chopin's *Funeral March* and danced the choreography she had dreamed the night before. Skene, too, remembered his own strange feelings that evening.

Back in Paris, Isadora sent for the six original pupils—Anna, Erica, Irma, Lisa, Margot, Theresa—all now in their teens and still at Elizabeth's school in Germany. Isadora did not yet have her own theatre, but she was preparing to dance at the Trocadero and at the Théâtre de Châtelet. Mounet-Sully and Rudolphe Plamandon of the Opera were to join the Colonne Orchestra in Presenting Gluck's *Orpheus*, and the Isadorables would be part of it.

It is a testament to the girls' love for Isadora and their own talent and courage that Darmstadt had affected them so little. Isadora found their dancing horribly stiff, but she began to work with them and soon they were ready to perform with her.

On the evening of April 18, 1913, Antoine Bourdelle and his wife were in the audience at the Châtelet. The sculptor was agitated and said to his wife that Isadora seemed to be dancing Death. She tried to calm him, but on leaving the theatre he saw Isadora's car pulling up to the stage door and mistook it for a hearse.

AT THE HEIGHT OF HER
FAME IN EUROPE,
ISADORA APPEARED IN
ROME.

The next day began as a particularly happy one for Isadora. Singer had returned and, longing to see her and the children, had suggested that they lunch together. Isadora had been staying out in Versailles to relax in the quiet of the countryside. With the children and their Scottish nurse, Annie Sim, she drove into town. Lunch was great fun, all disagreements forgotten, and talk was once again of the theatre plans.

After the meal, they separated reluctantly. Isadora had a rehearsal; Miss Sim and the children left in Isadora's long black car, to return to Versailles. They had not gone far when the car stalled and the chauffeur got out to crank the engine. He had left the car in gear, and when it leapt to a start he was unable to get back in. There were no railings along the riverbank—the heavy car rolled into the cold, swiftly flowing waters of the Seine. Attempts to free the children and their governess were useless; the current was too strong, and by the time the car was located it was too late.

PEN AND INK STUDIES
OF ISADORA DANCING
BY ABRAHAM
WALKOWITZ, 1917,
DUNCAN
COLLECTION

Isadora sat immobile in her studio while all Paris came to comfort her. Singer, whose heart was not strong, had to be hospitalized. Augustin brought the girls to her and at last, at the sight of them, she wept. "Now you must be my children." The students from the Ecole des Beaux-Arts, who had bought so many flowers over the years to toss onto the stage as they cheered noisily from the balconies, now came silently and filled her garden with every white blossom they could find. Mothers the world over, Elena Meo among them, wept with her and sent her their sympathy.

In her shock and sorrow, Isadora was still capable of composing a letter to the police requesting the release of her chauffeur, Masserand, who had been taken into custody. He was a father and she wanted him to be with his children. The Colonne Orchestra played in her studio as she knelt silently with Elizabeth, Augustin, and Raymond. From there the bodies of Deirdre, Patrick, and Annie Sim were taken to Père Lachaise Cemetery for cremation. Isasdora's friend the actress Cécile Sorel described the funeral procession:

Alone, Isadora walked at the head of the endless cortege. She resembled a mourner of ancient times. The people were crossing themselves as they followed the folds of her dress.

I wanted to kiss her naked feet in their sandals.

She had telegraphed to Craig. He did not come, but sent Count Kessler with flowers. He wrote beautifully to her in the weeks to come, but his first letter is the most touching:

PART III

Heroic: 1913–1927

Imagine then a dancer who, after long study, prayer and inspiration, has attained such a degree of understanding that his body is simply the luminous manifestation of his soul; whose body dances in accordance with a music heard inwardly, in an expression of something out of another, profounder world. This is the truly creative dancer, natural but not imitative, speaking in movement out of himself and out of something greater than all selves. — ISADORA DUNCAN, "THE PHILOSOPHER'S STONE OF DANCING" (1920)

▼▼
LA MARSEILLAISE
PHOTO: ARNOLD
GENTHE, NEW YORK,
1915

Isadora found herself alone. Elizabeth had taken the six Isadorables back to Darmstadt. The house and garden were silent—no children, no laughter, no dancing.

Raymond and Penelope were leaving for northwestern Greece to work with refugees from the areas devastated by the Turkish army during the war in the Balkans. They encouraged Isadora to join them, and in May 1913 she traveled to Corfu with Augustin. Paris Singer joined her there and tried to convince her that the last thing she needed was to plunge herself into the suffering of others. But the depth of her own misery sharpened Isadora's compassion, and she chose to remain with Raymond and Penelope.

Wearing a handwoven tunic and her plain sandals, Isadora helped to distribute supplies and settle the women and children in the camp Raymond had organized. His plan was to enable the people to become self-sufficient. He bought wool and designed a spindle that was easy for novices to use; he taught the women to spin thread and to weave. Then he sold their handiwork, and with the profits bought more supplies. Soon he was able to start a bakery, so that the residents could feed themselves, and to set up a school for the children.

In August, Isadora returned to Paris to do some fund-raising for her brother's efforts. She took along a number of the handwoven blankets and rugs to sell. Back in Greece, though, she began to realize that "there is a great difference between the life of

the artist and that of the Saint." Unable to bear living any longer in a tent among grief-stricken mothers and orphaned children, she left for Constantinople, taking Penelope with her for a short respite. A telegram soon called them back: Raymond and their son Menalkas were both seriously ill with fever. Unable to persuade Raymond to abandon his work, or Penelope to leave him, Isadora reluctantly left once again, alone.

Back home in Paris, Isadora tried to work with Hener Skene, but she could not bear to dance in her studio, where she had last touched the tiny cold hands. They drove to Italy, travelers without any destination but forgetfulness. She wrote to Craig, but he would not see her. Eleonora Duse sent word for Isadora to come to Viareggio. There Eleonora shared Isadora's grief and wept with her, listening to her recount every detail of her memories—her joys and the great tragedy. She also encouraged Isadora to use her sorrow to create works of art.

But for Isadora, especially now, "creation" meant one thing above all: a child. To this end she embarked on a liaison with a young sculptor. When she told Eleonora that she was pregnant, the actress was astonished both by her folly and by her courage in defying fate. One day Isadora danced for her — Beethoven's *Sonata Pathétique* — and Eleonora embraced her friend and begged her to return to her art.

When the women left the seashore in December 1913, Isadora and Hener Skene traveled to Rome. There they were met by friends. Gabriele D'Annunzio called often, but even the great poet and the splendor of the city could not distract her for long from her grief. Despite Skene's patient companionship, she still found it difficult to dance.

A telegram arrived from Singer, in Paris. He had reserved her a suite at the Hôtel Crillon. When she arrived, she told him of her pregnancy. Like Duse, Singer found this incomprehensible, but he accepted it philosophically. He asked her if she could put her personal feelings aside and give herself entirely to her work. He had purchased the Paillard Palace Hotel at Bellevue, overlooking the Seine west of Paris. It was his hope that in this magnificent edifice they could establish her school. Isadora agreed.

Louis Sue undertook the renovation, and in January 1914 the six Isadorables arrived from Darmstadt to help Isadora teach the fifty new pupils she had accepted. By April, Augustin and his second wife, Margherita Sargent, were accompanying Skene, Irma, and Anna to Russia to audition pupils for the school. They gave several performances to introduce the new students in demonstrations of various exercises, before returning to Bellevue.

As her pregnancy advanced, Isadora often taught from a couch. She had never been able to break down her choreography, analyze it, and teach it in small bits, and her six original pupils knew from experience that if they could not follow a dance, then her verbal guidance was sometimes more helpful. Working with Isadora and the older girls, the beginners made amazing progress, and many of Isadora's fellow artists came to visit and see the budding dancers. On June 26, 1914, the Isadorables performed at the Trocadero with the Colonne Orchestra. Mounet-Sully recited and Mme. Namara-Toye sang.

The garden at Bellevue adjoined Rodin's, and the elderly sculptor would sometimes come to watch her pupils dancing on the vast lawn or to walk with Isadora in the quiet of the evening. "Ah," he would sigh to Isadora, "if I had only had such models when I was young. Models who move and whose movement is in close harmony with nature. I have had magnificent models, to be sure, but none who has understood the

INTERIOR OF ISADORA'S
SCHOOL AT BELLEVUE

AT BELLEVUE,
ISADORABLES ANNA,
IRMA, AND THERESA (TO
THE RIGHT) ASSISTED
ISADORA IN TEACHING
THE YOUNGER
STUDENTS

IRMA, THERESA,
AND ANNA WITH
STUDENTS AT THE
BELLEVUE SCHOOL
PHOTOS: 1913,
BAKHRUSHIN STATE
THEATRE MUSEUM,
MOSCOW

science of movement as your pupils do." Her friend Mary Fanton Roberts quoted him as saying, *"Isadora Duncan is the greatest woman I have ever known, and her art has influenced my work more than any other inspiration that has come to me. Sometimes I think she is the greatest woman the world has ever known."*

Isadora had apparently risen phoenix-like from the ashes of her grief and was facing the future with assurance that her courage would be rewarded. Singer had taken the pupils to England for a holiday, and August 1, 1914, Isadora gave birth to a son. The infant lived only a few hours. This personal tragedy was mirrored by the sorrow of all France—the First World War had begun.

Isadora gave Bellevue to the Dames de France as a hospital and convalescent home for the wounded. The vast rooms that had echoed with the laughter and singing of little girls would now resound with moans. Her baby son was dead and countless other mothers would lose their sons. As soon as she could travel, Isadora drove through

130

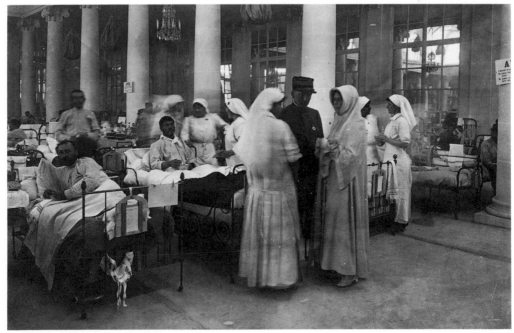

BELLEVUE AS A
HOSPITAL DURING
WORLD WAR I

ISADORA WITH AN
OFFICER AND A NURSE
VISITING THE WOUNDED
PHOTOS: BELLEVUE,
1914, DUNCAN
COLLECTION

the war zone to Deauville, where her old friend Mary Desti was working as a nurse at the hospital set up in the casino. Isadora read to the men and wrote letters for them.

As a number of Isadora's pupils were German, Singer felt that they might be unwelcome in England, so Augustin and Margherita took them home to New York. Elizabeth and Max Merz had also decided that they would feel safer in the United States during the war, and Elizabeth had enlisted Singer's help in moving her school to New York. Although Elizabeth had publicly stated the independence of her school in Germany, the two sisters once again found themselves teaching in New York where Elizabeth and the senior pupils took young pupils.

Isadora concentrated on working with her adult pupils, developing them as performing artists and as teachers. She established a new company called "Dionysion" in New York; in November and December 1914, the young women performed Gluck and Schubert. During her own absence from the stage Isadora had been perfecting ensemble choreography. Remarking on the beauty and freedom of the young dancers, the critic Sigmund Spaeth wrote: "This art which she has developed first in herself and now in others also, is more than a school of dancing or bodily exercise. It is a manner of life as important in its mental and spiritual as in its physical significance."

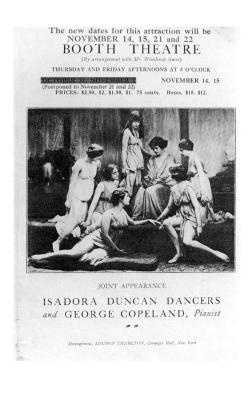

The new dates for this attraction will be
NOVEMBER 14, 15, 21 and 22
BOOTH THEATRE
(By arrangement with Mr. Winthrop Ames)
THURSDAY AND FRIDAY AFTERNOONS AT 3 O'CLOCK
OCTOBER 31, NOVEMBER 1   NOVEMBER 14, 15
(Postponed to November 21 and 22)
PRICES: $2.50, $2, $1.50, $1, 75 cents.   Boxes, $18, $12.

JOINT APPEARANCE
ISADORA DUNCAN DANCERS
and GEORGE COPELAND, *Pianist*

Management, LOUDON CHARLTON, Carnegie Hall, New York

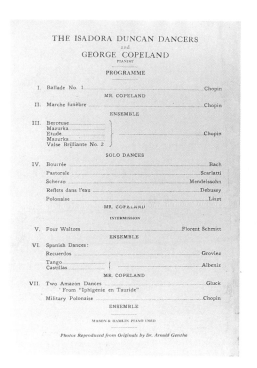

THE ISADORA DUNCAN DANCERS
and
GEORGE COPELAND
PIANIST

PROGRAMME

I.   Ballade No. 1 .... Chopin
MR. COPELAND

II. Marche funèbre .... Chopin
ENSEMBLE

III. Berceuse
     Mazurka
     Etude
     Mazurka
     Valse Brilliante No. 2 .... Chopin
SOLO DANCES

IV. Bourrée .... Bach
     Pastorale .... Scarlatti
     Scherzo .... Mendelssohn
     Reflets dans l'eau .... Debussy
     Polonaise .... Liszt
MR. COPELAND
INTERMISSION

V.   Four Waltzes .... Florent Schmitt
ENSEMBLE

VI. Spanish Dances:
     Recuerdos .... Grovlez
     Tango
     Castillas .... Albeniz
MR. COPELAND

VII. Two Amazon Dances .... Gluck
     From "Iphigenie en Tauride"
     Military Polonaise .... Chopin
ENSEMBLE

MASON & HAMLIN PIANO USED

Photos Reproduced from Originals by Dr. Arnold Genthe

At thirty-seven years old, Isadora returned to the stage in the spring of 1915. Her dances now were liturgical. Augustin's recitations were from the Psalms and the Beatitudes. Isadora had written to Hener Skene (who died later in the war): "I despair of life, but perhaps I can create something beautiful to dance during a Requiem, to comfort those who suffer as I do." One of her masterpieces was her choreography of Schubert's *Ave Maria*. As a solo, she danced the Virgin Mary: her acceptance of the Angel's Annunciation, the birth of the Christ Child, and her loving adoration of the infant. When the young women joined her, they danced a chorus of angels.

Ironically Isadora, who had dedicated her life to beauty and joy, who so deplored suffering, now created a great cry to arms. One night she danced the *Marseillaise*, to encourage the young men of America to join their brothers in France in the Great War. She recreated the heroic sculptures on the Arc de Triomphe. Carl Van Vechten wrote that "At times, legs, arms, a leg or arm, the throat, or the exposed breast assume an importance above that of the rest of the mass, suggesting the unfinished sculpture of Michelangelo." Arnold Genthe photographed Isadora in poses from the *Marseillaise* as the great warrior-goddess. And the public rallied to her cry. American support for the war grew.

Isadora addressed wealthy New Yorkers from the stage, saying they should be building her a theatre—preferably on the Lower East Side, where she considered her audiences more appreciative than those at the Metropolitan Opera House. If some were put off by her preaching, Otto Kahn, the owner of the Century Opera House, was not. He came forward to offer his theatre for a Dionysion season. Isadora set about making the large traditional house suit her tastes. She had the first ten rows of seats removed and draped the gilded boxes in unbleached muslin, to create a huge amphitheater. She priced the seats from ten cents to three dollars, with the greater number at the lowest prices to ensure that everyone who wished to attend would be able to do so.

The Dionysion season proved daring. It was the most complete presentation of Isadora's concept of theatre. The first program was Gluck's *Iphigenia in Aulis*, with choruses written by Louis Anspacher, and *Iphigenia in Taurus*, with choruses by the poet Witter Bynner. Those in the speaking Chorus were Margherita Sargent, Augustin's wife; Sarah Whiteford, Augustin's former wife; Helen Freeman; and Irma Duncan. (Isadora suggested that Irma Erich-Grimm, one of the Isadorables, be listed on the program as Irma Duncan.) The second program was Gluck's *Orpheus*. The third was Sophocles' *Oedipus Rex*, with Augustin in the title role and Margaret Wycherly as Jocasta. Isadora was the leader of the Chorus. The actors, singers, and dancers were joined by an orchestra and a 180-voice choir. Other programs were eclectic—Berlioz's *Childhood of Christ*, Bach's *St. Matthew Passion*, and the poetry of William Blake. The settings were simple; Isadora's preferred blue-gray curtains, and low hedges and flights of stairs reminiscent of Gordon Craig's scenes.

Unlike Raymond's historically based productions of Greek drama, Isadora and Augustin sought simply to revive the basic premise of Greek theatre: the unity of all the arts. Hiram Kelly Moderwell wrote an extensive explication, as if to offset any misunderstanding by the critics:

> . . . next Wednesday's performance does not pretend to the smallest degree of "authoritativeness." Rather, it is experimental, the result of impulse and intuition.
>
> It is just for this reason that it goes by the name of "Dionysion." For Dionysis divided jobs with Apollo. He took the responsibility of starting things, leaving Apollo the less pleasant job of finishing them. He provided culture and understanding. In Nietzsche's view, Apollo was the grumpy critic who sat through performances every night mumbling: "It's interesting, but is it Art?" Miss Duncan in her Oedipus does not expect to finish anything, but she does hope to start things.
>
> It is because of this faculty for starting things that artists are so peculiarly attracted to her.

TEMPLE DUNCAN,
DAUGHTER OF
AUGUSTIN DUNCAN,
AND HIS FIRST WIFE,
SARAH WHITEFORD
PHOTO: ARNOLD
GENTHE, NEW YORK,
1915

AUGUSTIN DUNCAN AS
OEDIPUS, WEARING
ROBES WOVEN BY
RAYMOND
PHOTO: NEW YORK,
1915, DUNCAN
COLLECTION

MARGHERITA SARGENT
DUNCAN
PHOTO: ARNOLD
GENTHE, NEW YORK,
1915

The critics preferred the dance to all other aspects of the production. The season was a financial loss, however. In addition to the enormous payroll, there were expensive details such as the massed lilies and roses that had graced the Easter programs.

It was at this time that the pianist George Copeland met Isadora. They agreed to do a series of joint recitals: not until the evening of the first performance did he realize they had never actually rehearsed together. In terror, he was on the point of refusing to perform when she told him simply to play as though she were not there; it was the music that was of prime importance. All went well. Isadora worked in her own way, but artistically the results were always sublime, and fulfilling to the artists who worked with her.

In May 1915, she decided to return to Europe. The older girls, now professional dancers, refused to be sent to Elizabeth's school in Tarrytown, New York, and Isadora agreed to take them along with her. She had hoped to settle in Greece, but the political situation there made it difficult. There was strong popular support for the Allies, but the monarchy was pro-German, so government support for a school directed by a vocal Allied sympathizer would have been unlikely. The girls were sent instead to a Swiss boarding school and Isadora took an apartment in Paris. Her salon became a refuge for

▼▲

**WATERCOLOR STUDIES
OF ISADORA DANCING
BY ABRAHAM
WALKOWITZ, 1917,
DUNCAN COLLECTION**

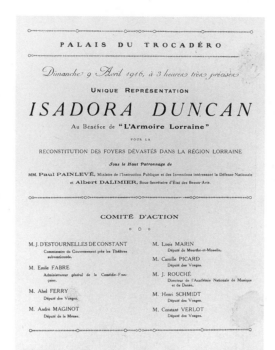

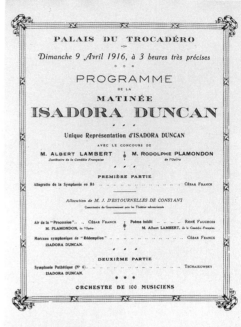

artists on leave from the trenches; with her usual generosity she made room at her table for anyone who came to supper.

Her return to the Paris stage in April 1916 was a benefit for the war effort, staged at the Trocadero. She danced César Franck's *Rédemption Oratorio*, Tchaikowsky's *Pathétique Symphony*, and the *Marseillaise*. The French national anthem had moved New Yorkers; now it was greeted with fanatical fervor by the Parisians. In her blood red tunic, Isadora was the embodiment of France, engaged in a deadly struggle. She was joined by a young pianist, Maurice Dumesnil, who had come to one of her soirées while on leave. He went with her to Geneva, where she repeated the program. This performance covered the cost of the girls' schooling, but did not leave her enough to save the contents of her apartment in Paris, seized for non-payment of bills. She did manage to save Eugène Carrière's paintings, which were an inspiration to her; but since the loss of her children, possessions meant less than ever to Isadora.

After a second concert at the Trocadero, Isadora and Dumesnil embarked for New York en route for South America. Augustin agreed to accompany his sister, but even he could not cope with what lay ahead. Isadora insisted on staying at the best hotels, drinking the best champagne, and wanted to dance Wagner—in the middle of a war she had encouraged others to wage against Germany. Dumesnil, on medical leave from the

Isadora's July 14, 1916 program in Buenos Aires was announced as commemorating the French national holiday. It began with the Argentine and French national anthems played by the orchestra and ended with Isadora dancing the French anthem.

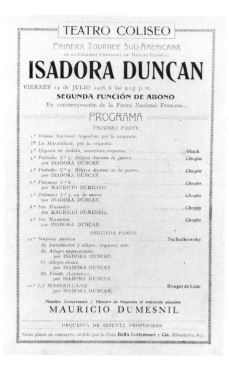

From a Drawing by Van Deering Perrine

Isadora Duncan
DRESS REHEARSAL
METROPOLITAN OPERA HOUSE
NOVEMBER 21st, 1916

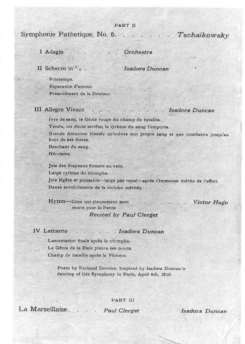

ISADORA DUNCAN
PHOTO: EDWARD
STEICHEN, NEW YORK,
1916, DUNCAN
COLLECTION.
REPRINTED WITH
PERMISSION OF
JOANNA T. STEICHEN.

142

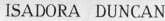

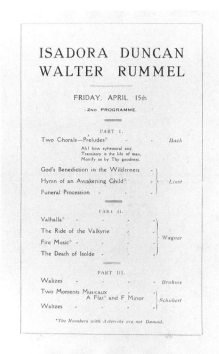

French army, of course refused to play Wagner, so an orchestra had to be paid to do it. Bungled arrangements and a dishonest manager along the way contributed to make the tour a financial disaster. The audiences in Buenos Aires, Montevideo, and Rio de Janeiro were enchanted by her dancing, but she came home empty-handed.

Returning to New York, she was reunited with Singer who was still in love with her. In November 1916 he rented the Metropolitan Opera House so that Isadora could give a free gala for friends, including Anna Pavlova. Isadora danced the same program she had given at the Trocadero. Singer then sent her ahead to Havana and Palm Beach, where he joined her for a winter vacation.

Back in New York, Singer gave a dinner to announce that he was purchasing Madison Square Garden (then vacant) for Isadora. She insulted him by asking flippantly if he expected her to have prize-fighting with the dancing. Singer had overlooked her many breaches of good behavior over the years, but this he could not ignore. Deeply hurt, he left the room—and her life—forever.

Why did Isadora insult the man who had been so faithful, so generous, and so supportive of her work? One can only suppose that she bridled at being beholden to her lover. But how sad that Isadora, who had so often helped those she loved, could not accept the generosity of someone who loved her.

RAYMOND DUNCAN'S
FOLLOWERS DREW
AMAZED STARES FROM
FELLOW PARISIANS
WHEN THEY WENT FOR A
SUNDAY OUTING IN
THEIR HELLENIC GARB

In a letter to a friend, Isadora made excuses for herself by asking, "Do you know what it is to have had three babies and now have empty arms? If you could understand, you would forgive?" Clearly her grief tortured her still, leaving her emotionally unsettled. She would continue to dance, to create masterworks of choreography, to inspire other artists; but her own personal life was reduced to an ongoing struggle to survive her great loss.

She spent the summer of 1917 with the Isadorables on Long Island. Visitors to their summer home included Elsa Maxwell; the surrealist artists Marcel Duchamp and Francis Picabia; composer Edgar Varèse; and the Belgian violinist Eugène Ysaye.

The girls took Isadora to see a movie for the first time in her life. She enjoyed it. Later she received invitations to work on movie projects, training dancers in Hollywood, but she felt that her art was not appropriate to the cinema. She refused to be filmed dancing. She was concerned that the movement would not be satisfactorily reproduced, and though she did not say so, she probably believed that the communion between artists and audience would be lacking.

Fall brought everyone back to the city, and to reality. Isadora rented a studio for the girls and set off on a tour of California. She had not been home to San Francisco in

RAYMOND'S PEACEFUL
COLONY AT MONT-
FERMEIL OUTSIDE PARIS
DREW REFUGEES FROM
MONTPARNASSE. AIA
BERTRAND STANDS AT
THE CENTER, HER HAND
RESTING ON THE WATER
JAR. THE PAINTER
FOUJITA IS FOURTH
FROM THE RIGHT.
PHOTOS: RAYMOND
DUNCAN, CIRCA 1917

over twenty years. She found herself in a strange city, reunited with her aging mother. San Francisco welcomed her proudly, and her performances were a great success. Ysaye had traveled with her, and together they attended a recital by the pianist Harold Bauer.

Bauer told her that as a discouraged young music student in Paris, he had seen her dance in a private salon and had been inspired. They planned a recital together. While rehearsing Chopin, they disagreed about the phrasing of one passage. Bauer played it—against his will—as Isadora insisted it should be done, only to discover later that the composer's original manuscript contained the phrasing Isadora had sensed. Like so many of his fellow musicians, Bauer had encountered Isadora's innate sense of musicality.

Back in Paris, she was introduced to Water Morse Rummel. A pianist and composer whose talent was coupled with a gentle and generous nature, Isadora found in Rummel a sympathetic and stimulating partner, whom she called her Archangel. He was ten years younger than her, but they were well suited. They decided to move together to Cap Ferrat, where they converted an unused garage into a studio and began to work.

ISADORA AFTER
HER RETURN TO
BELLEVUE

MARGOT, IRMA, ANNA,
ISADORA, THERESA,
LISA

THERESA, MARGOT,
LISA, IRMA, ISADORA,
ANNA, WALTER RUMMEL

LISA STANDING BY
THERESA, IRMA
RECLINING, ANNA AND
MARGOT SEATED LISTEN
TO ISADORA
PHOTOS: BELLEVUE,
1920, DUNCAN
COLLECTION

Isadora created two more dances of a religious nature, to the music of Franz Liszt: *Praise of God in Solitude* and *The Legend of St. Francis Preaching to the Birds*. She also arranged a suite from her previous Chopin dances to celebrate Poland in its tragic, heroic, and happy times, and the couple gave recitals for wounded soldiers. Unwavering in her loyalty to the Allied cause, Isadora still saw no reason to let politics influence her choice of music, and she continued to enlarge her Wagner repertoire.

Raymond had recently suffered the loss of his dear Penelope, who had worked tirelessly with him in Greece until she contracted tuberculosis. He now divided his time between Paris and Nice, helping to rehabilitate wounded and blinded veterans by teaching them painting and weaving. His community in Paris attracted a number of artists who sought a peaceful haven from the war. Isadora was now able to return the comfort and support he had given her in her grief.

When the war finally ended in 1918, Isadora and Rummel returned to Paris and sent for the girls. Isadora longed to have them join her in her new dances. Under Augustin's auspices, they had been touring in the United States with George Copeland. Now accomplished performers, they were enjoying considerable success, but their reluctance to give up such newfound independence was soon overcome by their desire to be with Isadora again.

Isadora had assumed that she would be able to return to Bellevue, but after four years of use and abuse by first the French and then the American army, she found it in a terrible state of disrepair. She attempted to raise funds to restore it, but finally had to accept an offer from the French government to buy it for a derisory sum. In its place she purchased a house in Passy, a pleasant residential area of Paris. The house had a small theatre in it, grandly called the "Salle Beethoven," and she hoped to work there with the girls and Rummel.

While waiting for the girls to arrive, Isadora, Rummel, and her friend Christine Dallies traveled to North Africa. They returned via Italy, and in Rome, Isadora was at last reunited with Craig. He described their time together:

> *We came together again for a brief moment in Rome (1919) (the night of December 12, Friday).... (This to the day 15 years after we first met together.) We walked & walked arms linked in the darkest Rome (it was as we passed an occasional shaded lamp, for the lights were dimmed in Rome, that I turned my head to see her dear face.) —we talked of nothings as we walked & again our hearts SANG—we were weeping as we walked but we walked all that way & ended smiling. Just to stand together was to us supreme intoxication.*

In the spring of 1920, Isadora danced again at the Trocadero. George Rabani conducted the orchestra, and this series of performances showed the full range of her work. One program presented Schubert's *Unfinished Symphony*, *Funeral March*, and *Ave Maria*, followed by Tchaikowsky's *Pathétique Symphony* and the *Marche Slav*, concluding with the

Marseillaise. Isadora had first danced the *Marche Slav* in celebration of the Tsar's abdication in 1917. The use of Tchaikowsky's militant music with its echoes of the tsarist hymn was mordant social commentary. Her portrayal of a serf in bondage gaining her freedom was Isadora's first explicitly political choreography. It remains as powerful today as it was over seventy-five years ago.

A second program was devoted to the music of Beethoven and Wagner. Approaching her forty-third birthday, Isadora was still capable of dancing an entire symphony and then *The Death of Isölde* and the Venusberg *Bacchanale.* Her talent, stamina, and charisma remained undiminished.

The third program was entitled a "Concert Spirituel." Cèsar Franck's *Rédemption* and *Panis Angelicus* were followed by Chopin's *Funeral March.* In the second part, Isadora performed "The Dance of the Young Israelites" from Berlioz's *Childhood of Christ* and "The Prelude," "The Good Friday Reverie" and "The March Toward the Holy Grail" from the third act of Wagner's *Parsifal.*

Craig was in Paris. After attending one performance, he wrote to her: "Never have I seen expression such as I saw two Sundays ago & to the end of my days I shall

never be able to forget it." He went to see her again and wrote:

Thank you dear so much for the dancing—I thought the scene & lights & all as good as they could possibly be. I suppose as usual these things troubled you a little—if so it was quite unnecessary for all was perfect.

Time had softened his bitterness, and all that remained was his great love and tremendous appreciation. Nor was he jealous of Rummel, whom he pronounced "a good fellow"—"she danced once for me while he played, & danced something superbly beautiful."

The girls arrived in late Spring, 1920—after the April–May Trocadero season—and Edward Steichen, who had made portraits of Isadora during her last stay in New York, decided to join the party as they embarked for Greece that summer. He photographed them dancing at the Parthenon. In Athens, Isadora set about rehabilitating

Kopanos, which had been inhabited by shepherds and their flocks since Raymond and Penelope's departure. The one large room became a studio where Rummel played while the women danced.

The death of the King, and the fall from power of Isadora's most powerful supporter, Eleuthérios Venizélos, changed their situation. There seemed no hope of establishing a permanent base in Greece, so they returned to Paris. During the spring of 1921 they performed in Holland, Belgium, London, and in Paris at the Théâtre des Champs-Elysées.

Even though Isadora called Rummel her Archangel, he was "more and more rapidly taking on the resemblance of a human being," as she noted. That spring, he fell in love with Anna. In their joy the young couple suffered at the thought of causing Isadora, so dear to them both, any pain, and as artists they deplored the idea of creating a rift in the group. They fought against their feelings for some time, but the situation became intolerable and at last they both left Isadora. Surely she understood and, loving them both, might have rejoiced for them had not her own need been so great. The loss of another of her "children" and a treasured friend and partner was a crushing blow.

Erica had returned to the United States to study painting and Margot was suffering from tuberculosis, so Isadora now had only three of her original pupils as partners. They performed that summer with Ysaye's orchestra in Brussels. In May 1921 an invitation came from the newly formed Bolshevik government, asking Isadora to found a school in Moscow. This seemed to be a dream come true, and she accepted immediately. Theresa, who was engaged to be married, returned to New York; Lisa was in love and decided to remain in Paris; but Irma agreed to accompany her to Moscow.

Isadora was reviled as a Bolshevik in America and her Russian friends who had fled the Revolution were dismayed by her decision. Yet Isadora was never political in the true sense of the word. She remained naive and idealistic, simply hoping that communism would lead to a better world—one in which children, and their parents, did not have to sleep on subway gratings and eat out of garbage cans. Isadora had tried to obtain government support for her school in Germany, France, England, the United States, and Greece. Praise for her work with her pupils was always lavish, but no government had ever been able to offer official support.

Leonid Krassin, the head of the Russian government's Trade Commission in London, had gone backstage to express his admiration after seeing her dance the *Marche Slav*. Isadora spoke, of course, of her desire to establish a school. Krassin had been so

moved by her *Marche Slav* and so impressed by her artistry in general, that he immediately contacted Moscow and soon came to see her with a contract. But she refused to engage in any business dealings and asked to have the opportunity to submit a proposal to the Commissar of Education.

Anatoly Lunacharsky was no dull bureaucrat but a playwright and critic, and on a visit to Paris he had seen Isadora dance. His telegram read:

COME TO MOSCOW. WE WILL GIVE YOU YOUR SCHOOL AND A THOUSAND CHILDREN. YOU MAY CARRY OUT YOUR IDEA ON A BIG SCALE.

Isadora responded:

ACCEPT YOUR INVITATION. WILL BE READY TO SAIL FROM LONDON JULY FIRST.

When Isadora and Irma arrived in Moscow in July 1921, they were not greeted by bloodthirsty Bolshevik ravishers, as predicted by the Russian émigrés who had tried to dissuade them from going. Rather, they found a country in the throes of political and economic change, where people welcomed them warmly but were sometimes unable to fulfill their hopeful promises.

Eventually they were allotted the former home of the exiled ballerina Ekaterina

Balachova. Balachova's husband was a wealthy tea merchant who had purchased the house from its original owner, Pierre Smirnoff: 20, Prechistenka Street was the epitome of Russian Francophilia, down to Napoleonic emblems amid rococo decor. The furnishings had been pillaged, making Isadora's redecorating task a bit lighter. Ironically, when Balachova fled to Paris she had considered renting Isadora's house at 103, rue de la Pompe, but decided against it because it lacked a formal dining room. Now Isadora was sleeping on a folding bed beneath the Napoleonic canopy of Balachova's master suite, rent-free. She awaited the relocation of the families living in the various main rooms, so that she could begin preparing the house to receive her new pupils, chosen from the vast number of Russian children who auditioned.

The optimistic Russian government, which had promised a thousand children and the chance to carry out ideas "on a big scale," now found itself embarrassed. Domestics and administrators were provided, but the kitchen staff often only had potatoes with which to work, and the administrators eventually had fifty pupils to oversee, not one thousand.

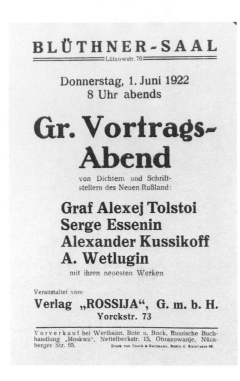

BLÜTHNER-SAAL
══ Lützowstr. 76 ══

Donnerstag, 1. Juni 1922
8 Uhr abends

Gr. Vortrags-Abend

von Dichtern und Schrift-
stellern des Neuen Rußland:

**Graf Alexej Tolstoi
Serge Essenin
Alexander Kussikoff
A. Wetlugin**

mit ihren neuesten Werken

Veranstaltet vom
Verlag „ROSSIJA", G. m. b. H.
Yorckstr. 73

Vorverkauf bei Wertheim, Bote u. Bock, Russische Buch-
handlung „Moskwa", Nettelbeckstr. 15, Obrazowanje, Nürn-
berger Str. 65.   Druck von Naack & Hartmann, Berlin O. Karlstrasse 40.

The school opened in October. In November, Isadora was invited to perform at the Bolshoi Theatre for the fourth anniversary of the Revolution. Lenin was in the audience and was deeply moved by her performance of the *Marche Slav* and the stirring finale, in which she was joined by Irma and one hundred children in the *Internationale*.

This invitation to the Bolshoi preceded the news that she would be free to give concerts to support her school. The government could not fulfill its promise of support: Isadora found herself in the familiar situation of being the sole supporter of her gift to humanity.

She chose to stay on in Russia and to work, as she had in the capitalistic West, to support her school. She had met the poet Sergei Esenin. Once again, she fell in love.

He was twenty-seven, the son of a peasant, educated by his grandparents, and had already made his mark as a poet allied with the Imagist movement. Already Esenin's friends had remarked how success had changed him, and it is debatable whether his attraction to Isadora was genuine or inspired by her fame. Since he enjoyed spiffy suits and unusual boots, did he simply want a mistress to match?

When Isadora planned an American tour for the school, she wanted to take her brilliant young poet along. Knowing that they would be confronted by social difficulties, she agreed to marry him. On May 2, 1922, they became Mr. and Mrs. Duncan-

ISADORA GAVE A SOLO
RECITAL ON THURSDAY,
MAY 15, 1924, WITH
THE ACADEMIC
PHILARMONIC
ORCHESTRA IN
LENINGRAD. SHE
DANCED THE SIXTH
SYMPHONY (THE
PATHÈTIQUE) AND THE
SLAVONIC MARCH BY
TCHAIKOWSKY AND
CONCLUDED WITH THE
INTERNATIONALE.
A SECOND RECITAL WAS
ANNOUNCED FOR THE
FOLLOWING SUNDAY,
AN ALL WAGNER
PROGRAM.

Esenin. The next morning they set off on the first passenger flight from Trotsky Airport, for Berlin. Isadora decided to introduce Sergei to the rest of Europe before going to the United States. The entire tour would prove a disaster.

Esenin suffered from epilepsy, and he drank to excess, which only exacerbated his depressions and violent tantrums. Unable to accept his position as the husband of Isadora Duncan, he wanted the West to recognize him as a poetic genius. Isadora attempted to have his poems translated into German, French, and English, and he gave recitals, but in general he was unsatisfied by his reception outside of Russia. He was abusive to Isadora and disparaging about her work. In spite of his unloving attitude, Isadora did everything in her power to make him happy, indulging his taste for flashy clothes and taking him to specialists in the hope of finding help for his worsening mental and physical problems.

Isadora had cabled the American impresario Sol Hurok asking him to bring her and her students to the United States since he had managed the Isadorables during their successful tours. He consulted Anna Pavlova, who confirmed his feeling that it would be a good decision. The Russian government, however, refused to allow the children to travel, so Hurok arranged a solo tour for Isadora.

News of Esenin's barbaric behavior had preceded them, and when they arrived in

New York in October 1922 they met with a cautious and confused response. Was Isadora a Bolshevik? One day she denied it and the next evening was shouting from the stage that she was as red as her scarf.

Her impromptu speeches from the stage became increasingly embarrassing. But her dancing, in spite of her own unhappiness, continued to inspire the greatest admiration. Her last American performance was on January 13, 1923, in Brooklyn.

Even Sol Hurok, left behind with the aftermath of the debacle, respected the artist. (In the years to come, he would present Irma and the young Russian women in the United States.)

In the summer of 1923, the couple returned to Moscow from Paris, where Esenin trashed their suite at the Hôtel Crillon. Back in Russia, Esenin left Isadora. The parting must have been a relief—not only to her but to the rest of the residents of 20, Prechistenka. For all the personal sadness Sergei had caused her, another man would contribute much to the professional joy and success of her Russian years. Lunacharsky had sent Ilya Illich Schneider, who spoke German, to act as interpreter and secretary to Isadora and Irma. Schneider was a journalist and critic who also wrote ballet librettos. He had seen Isadora many years before, and he hastened to greet her.

Isadora was also introduced to Nikolai Podvoysky, Lenin's close friend, who was currently organizing exhibitions of military gymnastics. He tried to enlist her collaboration, but never having been a gymnastics enthusiast, she declined. Nevertheless she admired Podvoysky, a very simple man, deeply. Standing with him on the Sparrow Hills, she pointed to what she considered an ideal site for a great amphitheatre. A decade later, the open-air theatre of Gorky Park would occupy that very site.

In the spring of 1924, Isadora went on tour in the Ukraine. She danced eighteen consecutive nights in Kiev to enormous crowds. She returned again in June with Irma, fifteen pupils, and a symphony orchestra. In the interests of economy, however, she decided to continue her summer tour as a soloist with piano music only. Her letters from the Volga district and Tashkent report squalid conditions and a lack of understanding of her art. She was elated to return to Moscow in August. During the summer, under Commissar Podvoysky's sponsorship, the pupils of the Duncan School had been teaching the children of the workers to dance. On her return, Isadora was met by five hundred children in red tunics.

Isadora now devoted herself to composing dances for her pupils. Her style changed a great deal in Russia. Her own dances to the music of Aleksandr Scriabin, the

Mother and the *Revolutionary,* and the harvest and hunger dances inspired by the famine in the Volga region, express the sufferings and anger of a mature woman. For the girls, she chose a group of revolutionary songs. The *Dubinishka* depicts workers hauling a rope as they sing. In the *Warshavianka*, the young women are warriors, each one seizing the flag in turn from the hands of her fallen comrade, until all lie dead, only to rise again. The dances, while often harsh and sad in subject matter, share a theme of hope, of ultimate triumph over adversity. Irma and the Russian pupils were equal to the material and their performances were called "overwhelming." This was the choreography of a harbinger. In the decades to come, dancers of social commentary and political protest would look to Isadora's work for inspiration.

Isadora's influence had already extended beyond the ballet in Russia. One of her pupils from Germany had married a Russian and established her own studio of plastique in Moscow well before the war. Ellen Bartells Rabenek had assisted Stanislavsky with choreography until she left Russia for Paris at the time of the Revolution. In 1923, another of her former pupils, Inna Chernetskaia, formed the Studio of Synthetic Dance at the Choreological Laboratory in Moscow. Chernetskaia's technique was also influenced by the ideas of Delsarte and Stanislavsky, and her aim was the synthesis of painting, music, and dance.

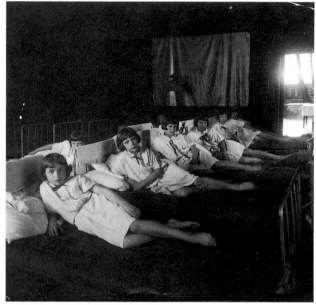

THE STUDENTS OF THE
DUNCAN SCHOOL

RESTING

PICNIC
PHOTOS: RUSSIA,
SUMMER 1922, DUNCAN
COLLECTION

THE STUDENTS OF THE
DUNCAN SCHOOL
DANCING IN THE WOODS

PLANTING CABBAGE
PHOTOS: RUSSIA,
SUMMER 1922, DUNCAN
COLLECTION

164

KONSTANTIN
STANISLAVSKY *(RIGHT)*
WITH ANATOLY
LUNACHARSKY,
MOSCOW, 1921
PHOTO: UPI/BETMANN

In Moscow, Isadora had the pleasure of spending time with her old friend Stanislavsky and again attending his work sessions at the Moscow Art Theatre. She now met a new generation of actors working with Stanislavsky.

Vladimir Sokolow was one of the actors who remembered his friendship with Isadora. He had first seen her when she visited the Moscow Art Theatre School during one of her early visits to Russia. Sokolow, then a student at the school, had been assigned to read a passage from Homer's *Iliad* while his fellow students expressed in gestures what they heard. He recalls that

> *As she was sitting amongst us pupils she could not miss the fact that all we were doing was nothing but the poor inadequate efforts of a bunch of immature youngsters. Nevertheless, she never let us feel that we really could not give her any kind of revelations as far as art was concerned. She accepted our efforts quite seriously and I can still remember her saying how difficult it must be for people living in our times, not only to get absorbed in the ideas of ancient Greece, but all the more to recreate them by acting and so bring them before an audience in a way which seems true.*
>
> *And yet it was possible, she said. Not by conventionalizing our gestures in the manner of a*

decoration on an ancient vase. That would only lead to more superficialities and would have nothing whatsoever to do with art. The means to an artistic creation we have to find in the depths of our own soul. Only when it becomes impossible for us to be anything but purely human will we be successful in recreating people who have lived 2000 years ago.

(INTERVIEW IN THE DUNCAN COLLECTION)

Years later, when Isadora was living in Moscow, just before going on stage one evening, Sokolow was astonished to learn that she was in the audience. He was playing in Alexander Tairov's *The Man Who Was Thursday* and his first feeling was one of intense disappointment that when at long last he had an opportunity to perform for Isadora, it was in a comedy. Isadora sent an invitation to the actor to come to her studio and greeted him by saying: "Do you know that you are a Tragedian?"

This was the beginning of my friendship with this woman. And in spite of the fact that I was an actor, not a mimic, I am persuaded that all I consider as being really important in my art, I have learned from her.

But above all there were two things she taught me: economy and harmony of gesture! Often she used to say: "A great thing you cannot express with a hundred gestures, but with ONE. Just remember how persuasive a little scarce gesture can be, born out of a great senti-

166

ELIZABETH DUNCAN
SURROUNDED
BY HER STUDENTS

ELIZABETH WITH *(L. TO
R.):* ANITA, DORA, AND
GERTRUDE DRÜCK
WATCH AS ANDREA
DUNCAN (AUGUSTIN
AND MARGHERITA'S
DAUGHTER) AND LUCIE
LEAD THE YOUNGER
STUDENTS
PHOTOS: SALZBURG,
CIRCA 1927, DUNCAN
COLLECTION

ment. An actor who spreads himself all over the stage confuses but never persuades us. How much can be expressed in the simple gesture of the hand in the act of giving or receiving. The act of walking, which should be as if your feet were kissing the ground. And think of the grandeur of a body in the act of rising from a lying, sitting, or crouching position.

But actors as a rule never stop to realize these things and only tire and confuse us with a hundred things, when one alone is necessary: Harmony of feeling. (IBID.)

Isadora was happy, working hard in Moscow. After a series of performances in September 1924 at the Kamerny Theatre, she did a command performance at the Bolshoi for the highest-ranking government officials. Anatoly Lunacharsky praised her work. Perhaps at last real support would be forthcoming. But there was the ever present need of immediate support for the school, so she signed a contract to tour in Germany. On September 30, she left Moscow. She would never return.

Elizabeth and a number of her students had returned to Germany after the war. Max Merz and Elizabeth's assistant, Gertrud Drück, had remained in New York to ensure that the school there would continue. But in 1925 they too returned to Germany to work with Elizabeth when the school moved from Potsdam to the Hapsburgian

STUDIO

D'ISADORA DUNCAN

343 - PROMENADE DES ANGLAIS - 343

NICE

VENDREDI SAINT 2 AVRIL 1926

A 5 HEURES

UNE SÉANCE D'ART RELIGIEUX

DONNÉE PAR

ISADORA DUNCAN

LÉO TECKTONIUS

PROGRAMME

NACHTSTUCHE .... Schumann.

PRELUDE............. Rachmaninoff.

MARCHE FUNÈBRE ... Chopin.

ADAGIO (PATHÉTIQUE) .... Beethoven.

IMPROMPTU........... Schubert.

AVE MARIA .... Schubert.

RECITAL ON RELIGIOUS
THEMES FOR
GOOD FRIDAY

castle of Klessheim in Salzburg, Austria. Like Isadora, Elizabeth now had students who had matured into teachers in their own right: Anita Zahn directed the New York school; Jarmila Jerbakova later opened a school in Prague. Isadora and Elizabeth differed in their methods, but they respected each other's gifts as teachers and they shared the common ideal of dance for life.

When Isadora's German tour was abruptly canceled, she went on to Paris in hope of earning the needed funds for the Moscow school. She was approached to write her memoirs, to publish her love letters. She wanted to write about her theories on the art of the dance; publishers wanted something racy. In the end she wrote the book that became *My Life*.

Isadora now divided her time between Paris and Nice. In Nice, she found a small studio and there she gave recitals. On September 14, 1926, she gave a joint recital with Jean Cocteau and Marcel Herrand. Isadora danced the poet's Orpheus. Cocteau then read some of his recent poems, one of them entitled "Danger of Death." A year later, to the day, Isadora would die.

Janet Flanner reviewed these recitals for *The New Yorker*:

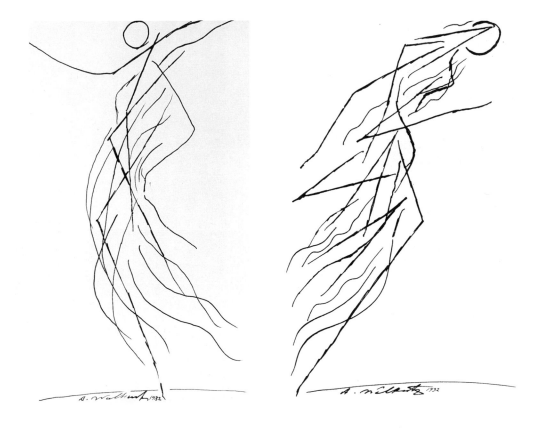

. . . her art was seen to have changed. . . . She stands almost immobile or in slow splendid steps with slow, splendid arms, moves to music, seeking, hunting, finding. Across her face, tilting this way and that, flee the mortal looks of tragedy, knowledge, love, scorn, pain. . . . By an economy (her first) she has arrived at elimination.

Raymond, who had taken one of his longtime students, Aia Bertrand, as his second wife, now had a daughter, Ligoa. It was a great joy for Isadora to be near her family once again. Ligoa remembers Isadora as a loving, generous aunt. Raymond thought that dolls were silly, but Isadora could not resist the pleasure of buying little Ligoa a lovely doll with a porcelain face.

Raymond and Aia had established a second Akademia Duncan in Nice. Raymond's brush-dyed and printed silks and cottons were now in great demand for clothing and decoration, and the ateliers in Paris and Nice were busy. The central motifs on the fabrics were painted freehand and the border designs printed from hand-carved woodblocks. Many of Raymond's students joined his collective household and everyone in the community worked together—not only on the fabrics, but weaving rugs, and printing books, as well as Raymond's newspaper *Exangelos*.

▼

AIA BERTRAND
PHOTO: RAYMOND
DUNCAN, PARIS, CIRCA
1918

AIA AND LIGOA
DUNCAN, AKADEMIA
DUNCAN
PHOTO: RAYMOND
DUNCAN, PARIS, 1921

THEATRE OF THE
AKADEMIA DUNCAN,
RUE DU COLISÉE, PARIS
PHOTO: RAYMOND
DUNCAN

RAYMOND WITH
WORKERS PAINTING
FABRIC AT AKADEMIA
DUNCAN
PHOTO: AIA BERTRAND,
PARIS, CIRCA 1920

RAYMOND'S STUDENTS
DANCING IN NATHALIE
BARNEY'S GARDEN
IN PARIS
PHOTOS: RAYMOND
DUNCAN

IRMA WITH THE
MOSCOW STUDENTS

MOSCOW STUDENTS IN
A POSE FROM THE
THREE GRACES
PHOTOS: CIRCA 1924,
DUNCAN COLLECTION

IRMA, MR. SCHEIN,
THE SCHOOL PIANIST,
AND STUDENTS, ON
TOUR IN CHINA
PHOTO: 1926, DUNCAN
COLLECTION

174

Although Isadora had difficulty living her brother's rigorous ideal, eating a strictly vegetarian diet and sleeping on wooden benches, she was always happy to be amid his inspired and inspiring artistic community.

Isadora had not heard from Irma in many months. At long last, a letter arrived. She and Schneider had taken their "Dunclings"—as the Russian pupils were nick-named—on tour across the vast country to Vladivostok, where, Irma recalled, "I used to drive to the shore and gaze out across the Pacific toward America. California, I knew, lay straight ahead." Having got that far, they decided to make a try for Harbin, then occupied by the Japanese. They received permission, and once over the border, proceeded to tour war-torn China. Isadora's art, truly universal, had encircled the globe like the embrace of her great arms.

In 1927, Irma traveled to Paris and she and Isadora were reunited. Isadora still cherished the dream of returning to her Russian school. She had applied for Soviet residency and it had been granted, so she planned to be back in Moscow later that year. In the autumn, the Soviet government undertook a plan to incorporate Duncan Dance into the public school curriculum. But when Irma learned that this would mean Marxist regulation of Isadora's art and Communist Party membership for herself, she feared

that the results would be a crushing of the "free spirit." Irma left Moscow and returned to the United States, where she performed, taught, and wrote.

Ilya Schneider continued as managing director of the Duncan School and the Isadora Duncan Studio Theatre in Moscow until 1949, when Stalin ordered it closed. Elena Terentieva, one of Isadora and Irma's original pupils, became the artistic director. While continuing to perform Isadora's dances, they also sought choreographers such as Leonid Jacobson to create new dances using the technique. Duncan Dance survived underground during the Soviet years, and today it is flourishing there once again.

One of Isadora's last real friends was a young Russian pianist, Victor Seroff. Anna Pavlova had introduced him at Cocteau's nightclub, Le Boeuf sur le Toit. The young man asked Isadora to dance, remarking that if he could say he had danced with the two greatest dancers of the time, they could report that he was a good dancer. Thereafter

Isadora and Seroff spent many quiet hours alone. In his biography of Isadora, Seroff wrote that there was never any question of his performing with her. He played for her privately, and she took tremendous joy in listening.

On July 8, 1927, Isadora danced at the Théâtre Mogador in Paris. It was to be her last performance. She danced superbly—all of her later, serious works. Seroff recalled:

Isadora told me that ever since she had watched Ellen Terry's and Duse's acting, she had learned that the true expression of tragedy lies not in the actress raging on the stage, or harassing the audience with wild screams, but on the contrary, in remaining absolutely mute and immobile when stunned by a sudden blow of fate.

"I understood that a long time ago," Isadora said, "but how to have the audience too feel it in the same way the actress does? How to make an audience stop breathing? How to hold three thousand people hanging with you on that one note which you musicians mark in your scores

with a fermata—meaning you can hold it as long as you like? Yes, to have your audience remain breathless as long as you yourself remain on the stage mute and immobile. That is true art, and I believe at that matinee I achieved it for the first time."

On August 11, a group of friends gathered at Isadora's studio in Paris to sign a petition protesting the execution in the United States of Nicola Sacco and Bartolomeo Vanzetti. They then marched to the U. S. Embassy to make their voices heard. Shortly thereafter Isadora traveled to Nice with Mary Desti.

Desti had been painting silk dresses and shawls in New York and had begged Isadora to accept one as a gift. It was one of her creations that Isadora chose as a wrap when, on the evening of September 14, 1927, she went out for a drive with a young mechanic who sold Bugatti racing cars.

Just as the car started, Isadora flung the end of her shawl over her shoulder. The long fringe caught in the spokes of the spinning rear wheel; the heavy silk tightened around her beautiful neck. She died instantly.

Raymond and Victor Seroff traveled to Nice to bring Isadora home to Paris. Her body lay in Raymond's studio, covered with her purple velvet mantle and an American flag. Then on September 19 he and Elizabeth led a great funeral procession toward the Père Lachaise Cemetery. There was an American Legion convention in Paris at the time and the Legion parade on the Champs-Elysées meant that the cortege had to pass through many of the smaller streets. Victor Seroff remembered that the people of Paris, who were buying and selling vegetables in the markets, repairing the streets, going about their daily business, stopped and lifted their children to their shoulders, weeping silently as Isadora passed one last time through the city. Thousands of mourners, famous and unknown, had gathered at the cemetery gate.

In the chapel, Ralph Lawton played Liszt's *Les Funérailles*. The Calvet Quartet followed with a Beethoven Andante and Bach's *Air on a String in G*, and Garcia Marsellac sang Schubert's *Ave Maria*. Isadora's friend, the poet Fernand Divoire, who had written so beautifully of the woman and her art, spoke a eulogy. During the cremation, Marsellac sang Beethoven's *In Questa Tomba Oscura*, which Eleonora Duse had sung to comfort Isadora after the death of Deirdre and Patrick, and Lawton played a Chopin Nocturne.

In a wisp of smoke rising into the autumn sky, the physical Isadora vanished. Her ashes were placed in a niche next to those of her beloved children. Golden leaves drifted softly from the shivering chestnut trees.

Today she stands silently beside all the performers who pause, before going on stage, to give their art and their bodies over to the power of their souls.

Isadora did not speak of "Duncan Dance." She spoke simply, with great reverence, of "The Dance." The art of the dance was sacred for her. She did not feel that her dances belonged to her, she felt that she belonged to the dance. Today, dancers who use her technique are called "Duncan" dancers. Many women have faithfully preserved her choreography and their performances are of great historical value. But the truest Duncan dancers are those who have followed her teaching that the work of each dancer must be unique—those who have listened to the music with their souls and created their own dances.

After Isadora's death, her friend Christine Dallies found the following statement among her papers:

RAYMOND AND
ELIZABETH AT
ISADORA'S BIER

RAYMOND DUNCAN AND
VICTOR SEROFF LEAD
ISADORA'S FUNERAL
PROCESSION THROUGH
THE STREETS OF PARIS
PHOTOS: SEPTEMBER
1927, DUNCAN
COLLECTION

Since the invention of the radio, we know that we are surrounded by music and by voices which come to us from all parts of the world. Our ears cannot perceive these sounds which the radio easily transmits to us.

I do not doubt that someday someone will discover an instrument which will do for sight what radio does for hearing, and we will discover that we are surrounded, not only by sounds, but also and invisibly, to our eye, by the presence of all that is no longer. The music and the voices that we hear over the radio do not cease to exist but travel in space indefinitely and, in time, attain other stars; therefore gestures also travel endlessly in space.

So, each word we speak, each gesture we make continues in the ether on an immortal voyage.

In this survival only, I believe, and that is sufficient.

"Dernière vision" (Last vision). Print of study of Isadora dancing drawn by José Clara after her death, Duncan Collection

Color Plates

185 COLOR PLATES

WATERCOLOR STUDIES
OF ISADORA DANCING
BY ABRAHAM
WALKOWITZ, 1908-
1917, DUNCAN
COLLECTION

WALKOWITZ, YOU HAVE
WRITTEN MY BIOGRAPHY
IN LINES WITHOUT
WORDS. I CAN PASS ON.
—ISADORA DUNCAN

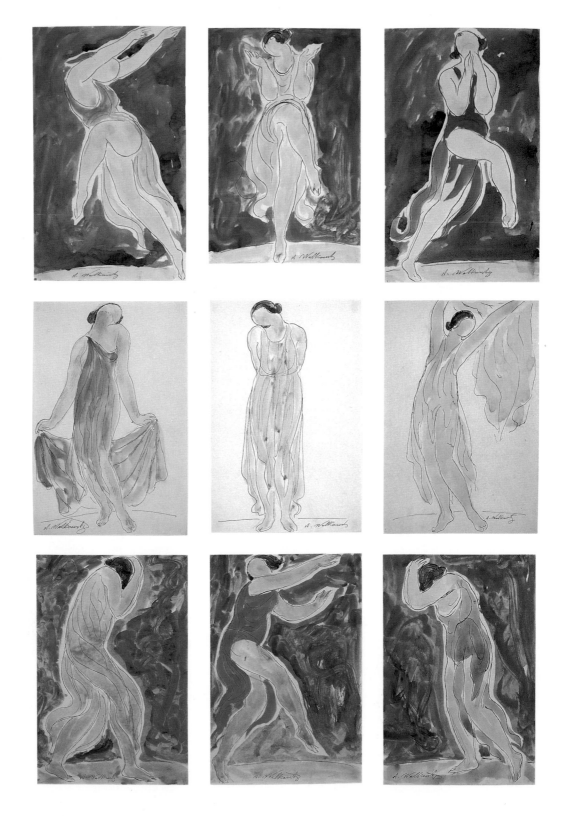

188

"BACCHANALE" FROM
GLUCK'S *IPHIGINIA IN
TAURIS* AND *VALSE* BY
SCHUBERT. PRINTS OF
CHALK DRAWINGS OF
ISADORA DANCING BY
JULES GRANDJOUAN
1912, DUNCAN
COLLECTION

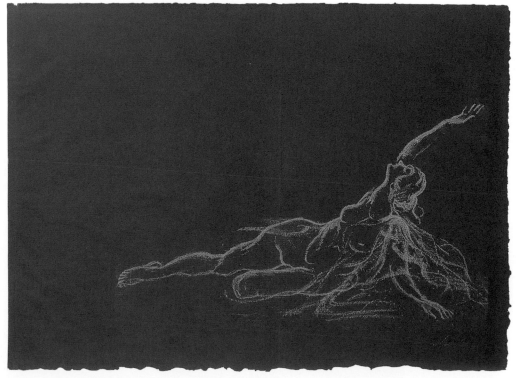

Color engraving of
Isadora dancing "Air
Gai" from Gluck's
Iphiginia in Aulis by
Mikhail Dobrov, circa
1910, Bakhrushin
State Theatre
Museum, Moscow

Ink and watercolor
study of Isadora
Duncan dancing by
Olga Mikhailova,
circa 1913-14,
Bakhrushin State
Theatre
Museum, Moscow

191 COLOR PLATES

Index